Grief Expressed

When a Mate Dies

MARTA FELBER

P.O. Box 1299
West Fork, Arkansas 72774-1299

Library of Congress Catalog Card Number: 96-94731

ISBN 0-9653967-4-6 (regular edition)

ISBN 0-9653967-3-8 (deluxe gift edition)

Printed in the United States of America

The poem *Home* appearing on page six is used with the permission of the author, Kay Winters.

P.O. Box 1299
West Fork, AR 72774

DESIGN AND PRODUCTION:	John Coghlan
COVER PHOTOGRAPHY:	Tim Ernst, Background
	Don House, Foreground
TEXT PHOTOGRAPHY:	Karl Sandrock, pages 38, 39, 88, and 89
	Don House, page 4
SCREENED IMAGES:	Corel

Dedication

TO JOE, my husband and best friend, whose death gave birth to this book—you taught me the meaning of true love and made our years together joy-filled. A part of you remains with me. . . . I love you.

TO MARGE, my "counselor" friend—you have always listened, but given no advice. Your faith in me has given me the courage to go on many times. Your positive approach to life is contagious. . . . I thank you.

TO KAY, my friend, whose love of life has inspired me to find my own joy in living—our joint adventures in faraway places provided memories to get through rough times. I applaud your writing successes. . . . I treasure you.

Appreciation

To the WIDOWED PERSONS in eight states in the U.S. who field-tested the earliest set of exercises for this book—the investment of yourself and your positive feedback encouraged me to go forward with the project.

About the Author

Marta Felber has drawn from her counseling background for self-healing after the death of her husband. Formerly, she held counseling positions in Bucks County, Pennsylvania, and Cairo, Egypt, and in Jakarta, Indonesia. With Kay Winters, she co-authored *The Teacher's Copebook: How to End the Year Better than You Started.*

Marta has three sons and four grandchildren. At present she lives in a Yankee Barn home on a mountaintop in the Arkansas Ozarks. She continues in her counseling role, with a focus on grief and loss. Another book, on leading grief support groups, is in process.

Dear Fellow Travelcr,

We who have lost mates are traveling the road of grief, moving toward acceptance of that reality. We are affirming our identities, apart from those of our loved ones. We are taking control of our lives.

Grief Expressed: When a Mate Dies contains the written work I completed on my journey. You are invited to journey with me, "touch my grief," and then do what is best for you.

These exercises were begun in a hospital room where my husband lay dying from a rare and incurable brain disease. Two spiral notebooks were by my side at all times. I wrote my feelings and how I might deal with the problems ahead. After his death I continued this process. The work I share with you is what I experienced and planned.

There is no one right way to work through grief. Each person must find his/her own way. WRITING my feelings and solutions helped me. It brought into focus the multitude of issues which confronted me. Later I could return to what I had written, for reinforcement, for direction, and to make additions.

You are free to use what I have written as a SPRINGBOARD for your thoughts and feelings. Also you may COPY anything from what I have written if it fits how you feel or what you choose to do. The moment you put it on your page, IT IS YOURS.

Resist the temptation to skip over a given exercise. Deal with ones from earlier stages and feel good about how you handled them. You may discover unfinished work you need to complete. Resisting an exercise in your present stage may mean you need to face it. Become familiar with upcoming exercises in the book so you can refer to them when you are ready.

Your situation is not the same as mine. DON'T GET SIDETRACKED by how I dealt with an issue. Make the exercises on your page FIT YOU. Change the title and headings to match what you need to do. Make up exercises of your own. Beginning on page 119, you'll find reading and resources for additional help. Above all, do the SUMMARY STATEMENTS at the end of every exercise. They pull together and make sense of what you have done, giving direction and instant replay for reading again and again.

Perhaps YOU WOULD LIKE TO SHARE in working through your grief with another person or a group. Additional copies of this book can be ordered on the last page. There is a tear-out, addressed letter page near the end for you to write to me about anything.

YOU ARE SPECIAL AND DESERVE TO BE FREE.

Marta

Marta Felber

HOME

Home was such a refuge
When he was there.
You felt the welcome
Shared the warmth
And knew the meaning.

Now,
Home seems like a place
You have to go
Don't want to stay.
Are glad to leave.

In time, you'll redefine
Rearrange
Reassess and find
That home is where you are
And choose to be.

Your refuge.

    Kay Winters

Step by Step

NOBODY'S HOME - And I Don't Want to Go There ... 10

FEELING SAFE - There Are Things I Can Do ... 12

WALKING "DOWN" TIMES AWAY - I Need to Exercise ... 14

I HAVE; I OWE - Where Am I Financially? ... 16

MY WORLD TURNED UPSIDE DOWN - On That Terrible Day ... 18

IT DIDN'T HELP WHEN THEY SAID - Those Words of "Comfort" ... 20

HELPS TO MAKE IT THROUGH THE NIGHT - It Seems Endless ... 22

EVERYWHERE I LOOK - There Are Reminders ... 24

WHERE ARE THE FRIENDS - Who Were So Close? ... 26

I WANT TO BE PREPARED - For Those Unwanted Advances ... 28

JUST SAY NO - And Make Time for Grieving ... 30

MY JOURNAL IS MY FRIEND - Always Near to "Hear" My Grief ... 32

HELP! I'M BEING BOMBARDED! - Disasters Hit All at Once ... 34

SAME TIME AS LAST YEAR - But Entirely Different ... 36

THE WORRIES GO 'ROUND AND 'ROUND - I Make Them Stop ... 38

FINDING STRENGTH TO GO ON - When My Feet Are Slipping ... 40

BUILDING A SUPPORT SYSTEM - People I Can Depend On ... 42

I TALK TO MYSELF - Making It Nurturing   44

GIVE UP (In Defeat) OR GIVE UP (In Release) - I Have a Choice   46

PROOF CALENDAR - Things I've Done   48

I NEED A HUG - It's Up to Me   50

MESSAGES TO SIGNIFICANT OTHERS - I Need to Say   52

MS. FIX-IT - I'm a Lone Homeowner   54

NEW FRIENDS - For My Personal Support Group   56

LONELINESS IS TO BE FELT - Alone Time Made Better   58

I'LL BE SEEING YOU - But Know You Are Not There   60

HE WASN'T PERFECT - No One Is   62

I AFFIRM MYSELF - Again and Again   64

I CARE ABOUT MY FAMILY - So I Put My House in Order   66

PUT THE CHERRY BACK ON TOP! - And Other Things for Me   68

THAT MAGIC MOMENT - The Story of How We Met   70

THE GUILT TRIP GOES ON - Unless I End It   72

WHO TAKES CARE OF ME? - I Do   74

DEAR JOE, IT'S ME, MARTA - Letters Not to Be Mailed   76

MAKE MY HOME MINE - I'm the One Who Must Live Here   78

LOOKING GOOD - Putting My Best Face Forward   80

A DECISION I NEED TO MAKE - Keep Francis; Let Francis Go   82

MEMORIALS - For Memory and Tributes　　84

A BREAK IN THE CLOUDS - That I Create　　86

MY MEMORY QUILT - It Keeps Me Warm　　88

THAT CAN'T BE ME - That Person Is Old!　　90

I NEED TO GO BACK - To Where It Happened　　92

I BELIEVE IN ME - My Positive Traits Are Still There　　94

PUT TO GOOD USE - When I Am Ready　　96

TO BE LIKE HIM - I'm Free to Choose　　98

SO LET US CELEBRATE! - I Count My Blessings　　100

TIME GOES BY - Nothing Gets Done　　102

THE THREE LETTER WORD - What About Sex?　　104

IT WAS A COMFORT - When They Reached Out　　106

WIDOWED, MARRIED, OR SINGLE - Where Am I Now?　　108

THE YO-YO YEAR - It's Been Up and Down　　110

IT WILL GET BETTER - That's What Everyone Said　　112

GOOD-BYES ARE HARD TO SAY - But the Time Has Come　　114

NEW YEAR'S DAY - Can Be Any Day　　116

RECOMMENDED READING AND RESOURCES　　119

LETTER TO MARTA　　123

WHERE TO FIND　　125

ORDER BLANK　　127

NOBODY'S HOME

And I Don't Want to Go There

The few things I needed were already in the supermarket cart. I looked at my watch. I had been wandering aimlessly up and down the aisles for thirty minutes, not choosing any groceries, not remembering anything I'd seen. And then I realized I didn't want to go home. Why should I? Joe wasn't there.

Ways to Make the House Seem Less Empty

Use a radio alarm to hear a voice when I wake up.

Turn on the radio before I leave.

Plan something pleasant to do as soon as I get home. Read a current book, brew herbal tea, call a friend, take a bubble bath.

Leave a light on for welcoming.

Consider getting a pet: dog, cat, bird, or, maybe, fish.

Invite someone to my house each week for coffee, a meal, or a project.

Buy some house plants and talk to each one. (It's supposed to make them flourish and grow.)

Interact with someone every day, on the phone or in person.

Change the area where he always sat, to make it look different.

Using a *TV Guide*, make a viewing schedule for the week.

Plan dates with friends and things to do to get out of the house. Try to balance these outings so I don't have too many days home alone.

Summary Statement: To acknowledge that I hate to go home helps me face the emptiness and do something about it. I can start today by doing some of the things I have listed above. I will check this list from time to time and add other ideas.

NOBODY'S HOME

And I Don't Want to Go There

How I feel about going home and the emptiness there:

Ways to Make the House Seem Less Empty

Summary Statement:

FEELING SAFE

There Are Things I Can Do

I never worried about someone breaking in or my personal safety while Joe was alive. That changed overnight. Suddenly I felt fearful and vulnerable. One of the first things I did after his death was to install a blind on the bedroom window. I lower it at dusk. Even taking such a small step to protect myself makes me feel more secure.

I Make It Safe

Install an additional security light on the house to shine over a larger area.

Keep doors locked both day and night.

Get a reliable flashlight and put in drawer by bed. Check batteries.

Consider an alarm system. Talk with people who have one. Research recommended systems in *Consumer Magazine* in the library.

Install surveilance "peephole" in front door.

Put 911 identity number at entrance to driveway.

Check into a cellular phone for bedroom and car.

List phone numbers of persons to call in an emergency. Have written directions to my house posted by phone.

Check availability and content of self-defense classes.

Purchase a key chain with pepper mace spray.

Put a can of flat tire fixer and flares in the trunk of my car.

Lock car doors. Park in a lighted area; pay attention to people nearby when coming or going. Consider a remote-control car security light.

Continue Automobile Club insurance.

Summary Statement: No one is ever totally safe, but as I choose to take additional safety precautions, I expect to gradually feel more secure. It is a relief to realize how many things I can do to help insure my safety. Many can be done immediately.

FEELING SAFE

There Are Things I Can Do

How safe do I feel?

Additional Safety Measures for Me

Summary Statement:

WALKING "DOWN" TIMES AWAY

I Need to Exercise

What has happened to my good health habits? An inner voice keeps nagging, "You've got to start reclaiming your body." I am aware of my loss of appetite, sleeplessness, fatigue, depression, and low energy level. I have decided to try WALKING THESE THINGS AWAY.

How Do I Get Started

FIND A WALKING FRIEND. My motivation is at zero. A partner would help. If I promise I will meet a friend at a certain time, I will do it.

START SLOWLY. I must listen to my body when it tells me I've had enough. Better to walk two shorter periods in a day in the beginning than one longer one. I can gradually increase pace and distance.

WALK REGULARLY. It is important for me to establish the habit, even if only for a short period. I will start with three days a week and then add more.

WALK EARLY. It would be a good way to get myself started in the morning. I find this very difficult right now. An exercise program will also increase my energy level for the rest of the day.

MAKE A RAINY DAY PLAN. Ride a stationary bike and read. Use an exercise tape. Mall walk, alone or with a friend.

SPICE IT UP. Use a Walkman and play music that has a rhythm which matches my mood. Plan something fun to do after the walk with my partner. Vary the walking route.

Summary Statement: I know I would feel better if I got regular exercise. It would add structure to my life. I would feel more like eating and also sleep better. It would be great to have more energy. Jan loves to walk; I'll call her and see if she can go walking tomorrow!

WALKING "DOWN" TIMES AWAY

I Need to Exercise

What an Exercise Program Could Do for Me

My Exercise Choice and Plan for Getting Started

Summary Statement:

I HAVE; I OWE

Where Am I Financially?

A bill arrives, and then another, sometimes several in one day! I start to panic. Is there enough money? Will I be able to pay my bills? How many more can I expect? What do I do if the money runs short? I must take time for a quick calculation of my income and what I owe. The reality may not be as bad as I fear. I also need a simple starting plan of action.

I Have   **I Owe**

Plan of Action

Place all bills, financial statements, requests for money, and anything else related to finances into a box or drawer that is used only for that purpose. Do this every day as soon as I get the mail.

Twice a month go through every item. (Pull out estate-settling items. I choose to get professional help with these.) Pay bills first, in order of importance. Make arrangements for any bills I cannot pay. Deal with the rest, all in one day if possible.

Balance checkbook and compare with bank statement on the fifteenth of every month.

Try not to worry about finances the rest of the month. If those nagging thoughts begin, I can say to myself, "I have a designated time for dealing with that."

Summary Statement: The above quick tabulation and plan of action will get me by for now. Most major financial decisions can wait until I can think more clearly and have the information I need. In my present condition I could make costly mistakes. I need to move slowly and deliberately and be in control. I won't let anyone pressure me into anything. When I am ready I will get help from informed persons who do not have vested interests. I am in charge of getting and using that help. Later, I will take a course on managing finances.

(See books on handling finances under Recommended Reading and Resources at the back of this book.)

I HAVE; I OWE

Where Am I Financially?

I Have   I Owe

Plan of Action

Summary Statement:

MY WORLD TURNED UPSIDE DOWN
On That Terrible Day

It had been gloomy and rainy for days, but the sun came out that morning. How dare the sun shine when he lay there dying and would never enjoy sunshine again!

Tell It Again, One More Time

It was a Saturday, but days of the week had lost their significance. What mattered was that he was still breathing, long past the time the doctors had given him to live. For five long weeks I had kept my vigil, day and night in that hospital room. I knew that it would be our last "home." It was here that I had made the hardest decision of my life, to sign for the removal of the life support system. It seemed as if I was taking his very life away. I had held out on this decision for more than a week, against the the counsel of his doctors and the reality of all the tests. Finally, I had agreed to let him go, and still he lived.

I did not know that it was his last day when I washed his face and combed his hair, as I had done every morning. I had long before learned not to expect him to know I was there or make any response.

I had struggled the night before, back and forth, back and forth, wanting him to die for his sake, and wanting him to live because I didn't think I could live without him. Finally, after many prayers I was able to say, "God will take him in His and Joe's own time. I can neither hurry it nor keep it from happening. I let it be." And, for the first time since his illness began, I was at peace.

It was as if he waited until I had reached that place of peace. He breathed evenly while I ate a few bites of the breakfast that the staff had brought to the room for me. Then I heard the irregular breathing pattern. The doctor had told me that this would be the only signal that death was near. I hurried to the bed and held him in my arms while he took those last breaths. I told him of my love, confident his hovering spirit would hear. . . . When my final good-byes seemed complete, I lowered him to the bed and pressed the nurses' call button.

Joe's life was over, and my life without him began.

Summary Statement: As awful as that day was, my one wish was granted, to hold him as he died. I look back on that day and say, "Joe's was a calm passing, and Marta, you did for him all you could."

MY WORLD TURNED UPSIDE DOWN

On That Terrible Day

Tell It Again, One More Time

Summary Statement:

IT DIDN'T HELP WHEN THEY SAID

Those Words of "Comfort"

During the early days of grieving, it seemed as if nobody could say anything helpful. It was not their fault. I was in such pain that I was quick to misunderstand words that were kindly meant. It is difficult to know what will be comforting when a person is grieving. Thinking back to those early days, I have recorded comments I remember and my inner responses.

When They Said	I Thought/Felt
"You're looking great!"	That can't be true. I feel dreadful. If I do look great, what's wrong?
"I'm so proud of you."	I must come through and act like I feel fine. That's what they expect.
"How are you today?"	Terrible. But I don't think you want to hear that.
"You must be really busy. I called you several times and you weren't home."	Do they think I am out socializing, getting over his death too soon?
"Let me know if there's anything I can do."	Please think of something to offer because I can't. I'm hurting too much to know what I want or need.
"You're doing just fine."	Am I being complimented for having "gotten over it?" Please let me grieve.
"Remember, it could be worse. He could have lingered longer."	What does it matter when he went? He's gone. Can't you understand?
"Joe is waiting for you over there. Some day you will be with him."	Maybe so; who knows really? I want him so much now. I don't want to die to be with him.
"I know just how you feel."	No, you don't. No one knows exactly how awful I feel and how much I miss him.

Summary Statement: Maybe I need to listen to what people mean, instead of what they say. Just accept that they are reaching out in the only ways they know, to show they care.

IT DIDN'T HELP WHEN THEY SAID

Those Words of "Comfort"

When They Said   I Thought/Felt

Summary Statement:

HELPS TO MAKE IT THROUGH THE NIGHT

It Seems Endless

I can pretend during the daytime that Joe is away, working outside or in his workshop. Alone for the evening meal and crawling into an empty bed confirm the worst! The loneliness for him descends like a shroud and there is no escape. What do I do to get to sleep easier? And what about those long hours in the middle of the night when I wake and can't get back to sleep?

Ideas for Getting to Sleep and Surviving the Long Nights

STICK TO A REGULAR SCHEDULE. Have dinner with the TV news commentator. Have a set time to go to bed, a radio alarm to wake me at the same time every morning. Get up, regardless of how little sleep I have had. Maybe take an early afternoon nap, not longer than 30 minutes; set the timer.

GET REGULAR EXERCISE EVERY DAY, but not within three hours of going to bed. Exercise relieves stress and may help me relax and fall asleep.

AVOID CAFFEINE AND ALCOHOL. In addition to regular coffee, there are measurable amounts of caffeine in chocolate, some soft drinks, and non-herbal tea. It is a stimulant that can interfere with sleep. Alcohol disturbs sleep patterns.

EAT LIGHT AT THE EVENING MEAL. Have a carbohydrate snack about an hour before bedtime. Also try a glass of milk.

AVOID SLEEPING PILLS. It is too easy to become dependent and too difficult to get off them.

GET SUNLIGHT IN THE AFTERNOON. Helps my body's natural clock let me sleep at night.

CREATE A SLEEP-PRODUCING ATMOSPHERE: Low lighting, soothing music tapes, tepid bath, deep breathing, visualization of a beautiful setting, relaxation of body muscles, or inspirational reading. Develop a nightly ritual of the things that work for me.

BESIDE MY BED for those long wakeful hours put dull reading material, a journal to record my feelings, note cards, a note pad for "To Do" lists, a manicure set, a radio for late night talk shows and music.

IF ALL ELSE FAILS, go to the kitchen and make hot chocolate, adding marshmallows. Sip slowly, listen to the night sounds, look for the moon, the stars. Remember that nighttime is a good time for crying, and crying is healing.

Summary Statement: I only need to get through one night at a time. I can do this. When I wake during the night, I will determine if I need to cry, get busy, prepare food, or just feel God's presence and a place of peace. Morning will come.

HELPS TO MAKE IT THROUGH THE NIGHT

It Seems Endless

Ideas for Getting to Sleep and Surviving the Long Nights

Summary Statement:

EVERYWHERE I LOOK

There Are Reminders

Why do I feel sad when I use the remote control? Maybe I know why. Joe always "ran" the TV while I watched and did mindless tasks. The remote is a symbol of all the jobs that were his that I had to take over, and that fact confirms his death.

Symbols and What They Mean

JOE'S CLIPBOARD. Reminds me of his profession, abilities, and special talents. How unfair it is that all were taken away. I grieve for his loss.

HIS COFFEE MUG. Embodies all our snacks and meals, his food preferences and eating out. Eating time is unbearably lonely now.

OLD SPICE MUSK DEODORANT. When he held me I was always aware of his "smell." How I miss all those hugs and close body times.

STATUE OF OLD MAN. He picked this out on one of our trips. It reminds me of our travels. Those times were so much fun! I mourn the loss of my traveling buddy and all the trips we had planned.

HIS TOOTHBRUSHES. How conscientious he was about taking care of his teeth. I admired that. Good health was important to him. So why did he get sick and die?

PLAID HAT. It hangs in the entryway and reminds me of all the things he did and enjoyed in the out-of-doors. I can see him on the tractor, gathering wood, and taking a walk. His hat gives me a warm feeling.

TOOLBOX. Next to me, he loved his tools best! He did the finishing work in our home. It still hurts to look around and see his handiwork, but some day it will be a comfort.

Summary Statement: From now on I will let the feelings come that surround these symbols. Only then am I free to hold these feelings or to let them go.

EVERYWHERE I LOOK

There Are Reminders

When I See (Objects)	My Thoughts/Feelings

Summary Statement:

WHERE ARE THE FRIENDS

Who Were So Close?

Our closest friends were out of the country when Joe died. The husband called as soon as they heard the news. After their initial expressions of caring, there was a dropping off of contact to almost nothing. I was so disappointed and hurt. This happened with some other friends, too. I am trying to understand.

My Friends Have Disappeared Because

They care about me and want to make it all right again. But they can't "fix it," and this presents a hopeless situation.

Our lifestyles are no longer the same. I am not part of a couple any longer. I'm dealing with probate, interpreting insurance forms, and wrestling with finances. They cannot relate to where I am.

Some people are not free to handle their own feelings, much less the feelings of others.

Joe's death is a threat to their own mortality. If he died, so will they. This is too difficult to handle.

They want me to be finished with my grieving and I'm not. Their time limit for me has expired.

My very presence is a reminder of Joe's death. It is more comfortable if I am not where they can see me right now.

They have not lost a mate, so they cannot possibly appreciate the depth of my grief. Earlier, I could not have understood either.

In my condition I don't fit into light social gatherings. I can't seem to pull myself "up," and they resent being pulled "down."

They think that finding another companion for me is the perfect solution. They try to set this up, and I'm not ready.

Summary Statement: I do understand why these friendships are diminishing. It is probably related more to the situation and where they are, than to me. A few friends have remained. They are treasured beyond measure. I am also making new friends who do understand. These select friends form a support circle around me. Later, I may reconnect with some of our former friends.

WHERE ARE THE FRIENDS

Who Were So Close?

Friends Who Have "Gone Away"

Why Have They Gone

New Friends and What They Mean to Me

Former Friends with Whom I Will Reconnect

Summary Statement:

I WANT TO BE PREPARED

For Those Unwanted Advances

No way was I prepared for those subtle, and not so subtle, advances from men in the early months after Joe's death. There weren't many, but they were unsettling. I want to know what to do if they happen again.

Advances	Ways to Handle
A man sitting next to me at the table inched closer and kept rubbing his leg against mine.	Change seats, if possible. Go to the ladies room.
Men let their hands linger at my waist or around my shoulders much longer than appropriate.	Remove the hand. If it is repeated, say, "Please don't do that."
Men make suggestive off-color remarks or jokes. They would never have done this if Joe had been there.	Ignore it the first time. If it is repeated, say, "I don't appreciate hearing that." Change the subject.

Feelings That Surfaced

Surprise	I did not expect this to happen so soon!
Invaded	I don't want him in my space!
Cheap	What does he think I am?
Angry	How dare he!
Defensive	Leave me alone!
Guilty	Have I given a message of wanting this?
Frustration	I don't want to deal with this.
Defenseless	With no partner, am I free game?
Lonely	It's so hard to go out without Joe.

Summary Statement: I need to take control of these types of situations. Being mentally and emotionally prepared will help me do this. It is also important to be in touch with my feelings.

I WANT TO BE PREPARED

For Those Unwanted Advances

Advances

Ways to Handle

My Feelings When These Happen

Summary Statement:

JUST SAY NO

And Make Time for Grieving

It's hard for me to say no. With the best of intentions, many people want to keep me busy. It's their "cure" for my missing Joe. I, too, thought I must get involved, and my calendar is filled. What I really need is more time to be alone and let myself grieve.

Just Say No To

Potluck suppers. (I don't feel like preparing food or making small talk. I would rather stay home with a good book.)

Singles Group. (The members are younger. I don't feel like joining in the discussions, and the social events don't "fit" me now.)

Bridge Club. (It is too complicated. I don't need the pressure of competition.)

An extended trip with a group. (Instead, I'll start with a shorter one.)

A dog. (It would be an added responsibility, and I don't want to be tied down now.)

A jazz concert. (It is not my favorite kind of music. Why should I go just to have something to do?)

Church responsibility. (Requires every Sunday preparation. Need to do something that is not so demanding, for now.)

Computer class. (I have wanted to do this for years, and I have the time, but it requires more concentration than I have now.)

Inviting the family for a holiday. (It will bring back too many memories to handle. Maybe next year.)

Hospice volunteering. (I must deal with my own grief first.)

Summary Statement: Each of the above may have merit for later. My first priority is to deal with my grief. I can say no to any activity that is not in line with my goal, without feeling guilty. I will know when it feels right to go ahead.

And Make Time for Grieving

Assessment of my activity level:

I Need to Say No To

Summary Statement:

MY JOURNAL IS MY FRIEND

Always Near to "Hear" My Grief

The pain is unbearable! I put down the feelings that engulf me. They come tumbling out, faster than I can write. Some words are blotted out where tears have fallen. I write the date and time of day before each entry, giving reality to what is happening. Sometimes I write a lot, other times only a sentence or two. Always I feel some measure of release.

To You, the Reader: You can begin a journal, writing your feelings on your page. Document with the date and time of day. Purchase a spiral notebook and continue writing, through your grief and beyond.

Why I Write in a Journal

My journal offers a ready release. It is always with me, going in my purse when I leave the house. My friends are not that available.

Having to write slows me down to a pace I can handle. It gets me off the treadmill of going nowhere.

My feelings get all jumbled. Writing helps me to separate them and to make sense of what is happening in my life.

Putting my problems on paper organizes them, and I can begin to write possible solutions. I can refer back and check progress.

When I need to release pent-up feelings, I can read what I wrote in the early days. That will trigger the tears that need to flow.

The questions that have no answers can be written down and then left on the paper. It stops them from going 'round and 'round in my head.

As the grief releases, I can begin to note some breaks in the clouds. That feels so good.

A running chronicle gives me a "then" and "now" to measure my growth.

My journal is the proof of my survival.

Summary Statement: This journal method of expressing my grief has helped me more than anything else. I will continue to share with my journal, as a friend who is always near.

MY JOURNAL IS MY FRIEND

Always Near to "Hear" My Grief

Date _________________; Time of Day___________________

Summary Statement:

HELP! I'M BEING BOMBARDED!

Disasters Hit All at Once

The gas serviceman man found a leak and said, "You'll have to dig up the line from the tank to the house." . . . My lawyer called and asked for two more documents, and I could not find either one. . . . The painter was coming to stain the deck the next day and the loose boards had not been repaired. . . . When I discovered ceiling tile coming down in the kitchen, indicating a leak above, I heard myself screaming, "I can't take it! It's too much! I give up!" I sobbed and sobbed.

When Disasters Strike I Can

Cry until I feel the tension go.

Find a physical outlet: pound a pillow, slam the bathtub with a towel, or go for a brisk walk.

Call a good friend and unload.

Back up and handle (or choose not to handle) each thing in turn. Make a list of what needs to be done. This puts me back in control.

Contact a logical person for each problem for advice and/or action.

Get away, even if it is only for a few hours.

Keep on top of each thing that happens as soon as possible.

Put the local and world disasters next to mine, providing perspective.

Summary Statement: I can stockpile strength during the periods of calm. I will also use those times to work on my "To Do" lists. . . . Bad times will come again. But when they do, I will share/release my frustrations and get specific help as soon as possible. These feelings of powerlessness will not last forever.

HELP! I'M BEING BOMBARDED!

Disasters Hit All at Once

Bunched together disasters that have happened to me:

When Disasters Strike I Can

Summary Statement:

SAME TIME AS LAST YEAR

But Entirely Different

I don't want my birthday this year! Joe always did such thoughtful things. But he died two weeks ago. How do I face my birthday and all those other special days without him?

MY BIRTHDAY. I planned the day—breakfast out, browsing time in the library, haircut and new style, birthday lunch at the nicest restaurant in town (with my book), and purchase of a birthday gift (padded cover for my exercise bike). The telephone was ringing when I got home. Friends near and far called with best wishes. In between calls I read the cards and letters I had saved. Missing Joe hit hard at bedtime and it felt good to cry. . . . But, I had survived!

HIS BIRTHDAY. Anticipating that his birthday would be harder than mine, I had chosen this time for my friend to come from out of state. We went to Joe's favorite Mexican restaurant, where we toasted him with margaritas. I kept thinking, "The only way out is through." In between the tears I talked constantly about Joe, and my friend listened. I ordered his old stand-by meal. It seemed as if he should be sitting there in the booth with us. It hurt, but I'm glad we went.

OUR ANNIVERSARY. For months I dreaded the day. Should I pretend that it was any other day or plow right through the grief I felt? I chose to make it special and remember. My son agreed to go with me to the lovely restaurant where Joe and I had celebrated our anniversary many times. As the waitress got closer to the drapery-drawn private booth, I wanted to shout, "No, that booth is Joe's and mine!" I couldn't believe that we could sit through that long meal (in the booth that Joe and I always asked for), swap stories about Joe that the other had not heard, and not feel sad. Sometimes we laughed. Before going to bed that night, I read the cards that Joe had saved. They confirmed that I had told him over and over how much he meant to me. The day I had dreaded so much had turned out to be both beautiful and special.

THANKSGIVING. I took care of this holiday by working at the Salvation Army serving dinner to needy persons. Joe and I had talked about doing this but never had. I worked this year for both of us.

CHRISTMAS. I knew I couldn't stay in our home for Christmas that first year without Joe. After my "have-to" list was done, I ran away to Hot Springs, Arkansas, and stayed for three days in a hotel. I indulged myself in the famous hot springs baths and got a massage. A Christmas Eve service on TV and telephone time with my family on Christmas Day was all of the holiday that I could handle. The rest of the time I read, cried, and ate chocolates. I allowed Christmas to flow around me that year. It was the best that I could do.

Summary Statement: For each special day I need to determine what I can and cannot handle. Then I plan, plan, plan. Dreading the days does not help and may be unwarranted. Each special day survived helps me to face the next one. I will start new rituals and traditions.

SAME TIME AS LAST YEAR
But Entirely Different

How I Handled or Will Handle:

Birthdays

Our Anniversary

Thanksgiving

Christmas

Other Special Days

Summary Statement:

THE WORRIES GO 'ROUND AND 'ROUND

I Make Them Stop

The box I was carrying down the stairs required two hands. I tripped and almost fell. I found myself trembling! What if I had fallen and really hurt myself? I could have laid there for days before someone found me. Worries about health, safety, and other matters go 'round in my head. I'll write them on the Worry Wheel and put it away. In a few months I'll see what happened to my worries. Today's date __February 2__

Rim of Truth date __August 4__ (six months later)

Summary Statement: The Rim of Truth shows me that most of my worries have not come true. So why worry? Worries held on to become more entrenched. When a worry hits, I ask, "What can I do about this?" Then I DO SOMETHING or LET IT GO!

THE WORRIES GO 'ROUND AND 'ROUND

I Make Them Stop

Write a worry that you have in each of the spokes of the wheel below. Choose ones which seem to go 'round and 'round in your head. Remember little ones as well as big ones. Try to put one in every spoke. Do not write in the outside rim of the wheel.

Worry Wheel date ___________________

Later write in the Rim of Truth what happened to each worry. Rim of Truth date _______________

Summary Statement:

FINDING STRENGTH TO GO ON

When My Feet Are Slipping

Sometimes grief washes over me like waves, and I scramble for something solid. What can I count on?

I Believe

There is a God who cares about me and is with me all the time.

The sun will rise and set.
Spring will follow winter.
New life will emerge from buried bulbs.

My closest friends love and accept me as I am.

I am a worthwhile person.
I am intelligent, capable, with inner strengths.

Tomorrow is a new day.

My Beliefs Can Be Posted On

The mirror of my dressing table.

A stand-up card on the table where I eat.

A card to use as a bookmark.

The frame of the computer screen.

The door of the microwave.

Summary Statement: As I stand on these beliefs, I can withstand the storms that will come.

FINDING STRENGTH TO GO ON
When My Feet Are Slipping

I Believe

My Beliefs Can Be Posted On

Summary Statement:

BUILDING A SUPPORT SYSTEM

People I Can Depend On

I need people in my life, for companionship, advice, and getting things done.

I Have Someone For

Repairs around the house: Karl (son), Jim (handyman).

Home care decisions: Don (neighbor).

Car maintenance: Jim (keeps twenty-seven-year-old "Francis" running smoothly).

Family problem sharing: Marge, Kay (long-term friends).

Companion for plays, lectures, concerts: Edith (new widow friend).

Travel companion: Rozetta (who has been many places).

Elderhostel participant: Betty (we attended our first one together).

Exercise coordinator: Pat (water aerobics in her pool).

Financial help: Jim (broker), Walter (CPA).

Legal assistance: Jim (lawyer).

Landscaping: LeAnn (does "natural" landscaping that I like).

Hair care: Robert (created my new hair style).

Eating-out friend: Jan (enjoys eating leisurely).

Shopping comrade: Neva (appreciates finding great bargains too).

Weight control partner: Peggy (monthly weigh-ins and inspiration).

Daily contact person in the outside world: Willa (Postmistress).

Good book recommendation: Juanita (Librarian).

Chairman of my Fan Club: Marlene (thinks I'm wonderful and tells me).

Loving letter writer: Hilde (from the other side of the world).

Emergency contact: Karl (son: name, address, phone is in my wallet).

Medical consultant: Dr. Cude (family doctor for many years).

Life-line to Joe: Troy and Suzy (Joe's nephew and his wife).

Summary Statement: I have so many people on whom I can depend! I will add to this list as needs arise. For now it is OK to get all the help I can.

BUILDING A SUPPORT SYSTEM

People I Can Depend On

I Have Someone For

Summary Statement:

I TALK TO MYSELF

Making It Nurturing

It was cold in the mall parking lot, and the wind made it seem even colder. I half stumbled up and down the rows of parked cars searching for mine. As I walked I talked to myself. "Stupid! You can't remember anything! What's the matter with you? All you had to do was fix a landmark. You'll never find it if you start crying!" Later as I sat in the car, I continued to hear the negative words.

Negative Talk

On a separate sheet I will keep a running list of self-criticisms and put-downs as I become aware of them.

Nurturing Conversations with Myself

There is much on your mind. . . . It's easy to forget. . . . Perhaps next time you'll look for a landmark. . . . It's OK. . . . Give yourself time. . . . Your friends still love you, regardless of what you do that seems strange. . . . Try again later to balance your checkbook. . . . It's OK to cry, even in front of others. . . . You can't expect to handle everything alone; ask for help. . . . Other people run out of gas, too, and they don't have your distractions. . . . It really hurts when people no longer write or call as much as they did earlier. . . . Put the form away until you feel more like filling it out. . . . Your son will understand that you forgot his birthday this year. . . . You will begin getting out more when you feel like it. . . . Don't expect your health to be what it was before. Just take care of yourself. . . . Pace yourself and give yourself more time to get things done. . . . You seem stronger today. . . . It's OK to be angry. Find acceptable ways to let it out. . . . Set small goals. Feel good about reaching any. . . . Nobody's perfect. Allow yourself some failures and mistakes. . . . Contain your periods of depression and feeling sorry for yourself. When the time is up, bring yourself out and get busy. . . . You did the best you could; let the guilt go. . . . What you keep calling "excuses" are actually reasons why you are feeling and behaving the way you are. Accept and understand. . . . Being late a few times is not a catastrophe. . . . Sit down and recall where you last had your keys. Retrace your steps and you will probably find them. . . . Trust yourself. You will know when it is time to reach out. . . . You have inner beauty that will show more and more. . . . It is all right for you to say that you won't accept another volunteer job. You know what you can handle. . . . You are discouraged that you are not through your grieving. Be patient. Everyone grieves in his/her own way and own time. . . . It's OK that your needs come first for now. . . . Expect some disorientation from time to time. You will come out of it. . . . You made decisions before; you will make them again. . . . It's fine to treat yourself. . . . You are a survivor. Visualize yourself as a survivor. . . . Trust yourself to do the things you need to do.

Summary Statement: The way I treat myself is more important than what anyone else says about me or does to me. I am with myself twenty-four hours a day. I will become more kind, loving, forgiving, supportive, and firm toward myself.

I TALK TO MYSELF
Making It Nurturing

Some Negative Talk I've Directed toward Myself

Nurturing Things I Need to Say

Summary Statement:

GIVE UP (In Defeat) OR GIVE UP (In Release)

I Have a Choice

How easy it would be to give up. Some days I do. But that feels worse than trying to go on. Is there no way out? Below, I face my defeating attitudes and attempt to release the pain that perpetuates them.

Give Up (In Defeat)	Give Up (In Release)
I don't want to go on living without him.	I understand. Our times together held such meaning. He is gone. I let him go. My life continues.
I don't care what happens to me.	I let go of the claim on my life I gave to him. I proclaim my worth, separate from him.
The "If-only-I-had's" go 'round and 'round.	Where I need forgiveness, I forgive. I did the best I could.
There is too much to manage alone.	I resent being left to handle everything. I release the resentment and get the help I need.
I can't bear to think about him or our times together.	I keep the beautiful memories where I can bring them out when I choose. I do not let them engulf me.
It was devastating the way he died. A part of me died, too.	After much retelling, I will exorcise the horrible time of his illness and death.
I'll never get over this.	I feel deep pain; I let it go.
There will never be another relationship as fulfilling.	There won't be another relationship exactly the same. I keep my heart open to the future.

Summary Statement: I could give up, but I choose to go on. When the defeating times come, I will return to this page, review what I have written, and continue the process I have begun.

GIVE UP (In Defeat) or GIVE UP (In Release)

I Have a Choice

Give Up (In Defeat)   **Give Up (In Release)**

Summary Statement:

PROOF CALENDAR

Things I've Done

Every day I record something I have done, however small. It is proof that I am functioning and in control of my life. At the end of each week, I will read all the entries for that week. The last day of the month, I'll skim the entire page and feel good about my accomplishments. Then I'll make a new calendar for the next month and keep going.

SUNDAY	MONDAY	TUESDAY	WEDNESDAY	THURSDAY	FRIDAY	SATURDAY
	1 Made some dates ahead with friends.	**2** Packed box of Joe's things to send to his son.	**3** Defrosted freezer, a job I hate.	**4** Substituted Power Bar for high fat Mexican Restaurant.	**5** Called Jan and made time to walk at her house.	**6** Relaxed and watched fun video with son.
7 Weather bad. Stayed home from church and didn't feel guilty.	**8** Registered for a workshop on handling grief.	**9** "Modeled" four dresses in a style show at a luncheon.	**10** Picked up in house so it looks fairly decent all over.	**11** Curled up in front of fire. Read, slept and cried a little.	**12** Wrote difficult letter to son that I have been putting off for months.	**13** Had low fat lunch at mall with Peggy.
14 Leisurely brunch with Edith after early church.	**15** Wrote long letter to Joe about guilty feelings.	**16** Cleaned out clothes closet.	**17** Listed, packed clothes and put in car, ready to go to Salvation Army.	**18** Called friend whose brother just died. Listened for an hour.	**19** Splurged on a body massage. So relaxing!	**20** Went on long hike with Edith.
21 Went to Singles S.S. Class for the first time.	**22** Found someone to call about heating problem.	**23** Refused delicious looking German chocolate cake at luncheon.	**24** Got car serviced, before overdue.	**25** Found some pictures of us. Cried myself to sleep. That's O.K.	**26** Worked on putting pictures in a photo album.	**27** Remembered re-cycling day.
28 Visited Ralph in Rehab Center after church.	**29** Rode extra fifteen minutes on stationery bike.	**30** Made big mistake, but stopped myself from beating on me. Was understanding.	**31** Fixed nice meal for myself tonight. Lit candles.			

YOUR CALENDAR is on the following page. Make a number of copies before you begin. Take one copy and fill in the dates to match this month. Begin recording something you do, or don't do, each day, about which you feel positive. Nothing can be too insignificant to count. Reread later and feel YOUR CONTROL of your life.

MONTH ____   YEAR____________

SUNDAY	MONDAY	TUESDAY	WEDNESDAY	THURSDAY	FRIDAY	SATURDAY

I NEED A HUG

It's Up to Me

There were lots of hugs in the beginning, an acceptable way for people to show their caring. They no longer remember to do this and I miss Joe's hugs even more. I guess it is up to me. I can give a hug and get one in return. Or I can simply say, "I need a hug today."

Little "Hugs" I Can Give Myself

BREAKFAST IN BED. The bed is still warm. And who cares if a few crumbs get scattered around when I eat my toast?

SELECTED MUSIC. Invest in some tapes of relaxing background music, with no lyrics to jar back memories.

COMFORT DRINKS. Have a variety for all through the day, ending with hot chocolate and miniature marshmallows at bedtime.

ROCKING CHAIR. I rocked my children; I'll try it for me. With the chair facing a window, I can look out and be in the sunshine.

PHONE LIFELINE. With a few selected persons, I can share all my heartaches and feel their unconditional love.

BOOKS. Old favorites are what I choose to read now. It's almost like being with a long lost friend.

AFGHAN. I like to feel the afghan my aunt made tucked tightly around me, even when I'm not cold. Her love surrounds me.

WARM BATH. I let anxieties melt away, relaxing as long as I like.

BED WARMER. Five minutes with the electric blanket turned on warms the bed and makes me feel more welcome there.

WORDS OF COMFORT. Reading a few verses from a book of inspirational writings brings peace at the end of my day.

HIS PILLOW. I hold his pillow and go to sleep.

Summary Statement: My body craves hugs. I ask for hugs from others and I give them to myself.

I NEED A HUG

It's Up to Me

My Current "Hug Level:"

Little Hugs I Can Give Myself

Summary Statement:

MESSAGES TO SIGNIFICANT OTHERS

I Need to Say

It was the day after the services. With utmost confidence my oldest son assured me, "Mom, I know you're strong. You're going to handle this like you've dealt with everything else in your life." I wanted to scream, "But this is different! How can I live without him?" . . . What are the messages I need to say to my family and close friends?

OLDEST SON. I do need your continued support and caring through my time of grief. Allow me to "not cope." . . . The week you stayed after everyone else had gone meant more than I can say. Maybe the jobs you finished were done for Joe as well as for me. You loved him too. . . . How you hated to leave me home alone. Then I found the caring letter you had left. As I read it and cried, I felt your arms still around me.

MIDDLE SON. Joe's death does not mean you will have to deal with your wife's death soon. When/if that time comes, you will find the strength. Death is a fact of life and must be accepted. . . . Much of the time you hold your feelings inside. When Joe died you were able to tell me and show me how much you cared. I'm glad. Your calls have meant so much.

YOUNGEST SON. It's OK to talk about Joe's death and cry. We can do this together. Even though you are close by, I do not expect you to take Joe's place, in any way. I do need your help, and I appreciate your willingness, but I do not expect you to do all the work he did. . . . I want you to feel free to move away from this area when the time is right for you. Trust me to survive when you need to go.

SISTER. It means so much to hear you say, "I pray for you every day." I do feel your prayers and your love. . . . Being sixteen years older, you always seemed like a mother to me, and I used to resent feeling that way. In the past few years, I've come to an understanding of what your life was like and your need to be the way you are. No longer do I need to act like a rebelling teenager. I am now free to love you and provide care during your progressing illness.

CLOSE FRIEND. You came and listened for ten days! I poured out the whole story of Joe's illness and death. When I thought I was finished, I still found more. After you left, I was able to dream about Joe for the first time since his death. They were healthy dreams, a tribute to our grief work together. Thank you for listening and caring.

CLOSE FRIEND. The poems you wrote just for me I will always treasure. Almost every day I could count on a cheery postcard, a note, a call, a tiny gift from you. As I expected, messages from others dwindled to a halt. But yours have continued to the present. I know you will always be there for me.

Summary Statement: Putting my thoughts on paper has helped me focus what I want to say to significant persons in my life. I will convey these messages by letter, phone, or in person.

SAGES TO SIGNIFICANT OTHERS

I Need to Say

SAGES TO SIGNIFICANT OTHERS

I Need to Say

MS. FIX-IT

I'm a Lone Homeowner

Joe liked to fix things so much that I would tease him, "I believe you break things just so you can repair them!" Although I do know the difference between a Phillips screwdriver and a regular one, I never had to hold one in my hand when Joe was around. NOW what do I do? What are the bare basics?

Tool Kit Kept in Special Place

Can of WD-40
Screwdrivers, regular and Phillips
Pliers (insulated)
Kit assortment of screws, nuts, bolts, nails
Vice grip (small pair)
Pen flashlight with spare batteries
Electrical tape
Picture hangers
Measuring tape, ruler

Know Location and Operation Of

Water cut-off valves
Electrical fuse boxes in house
Generator backup for furnace
Sewer system
Gas tank meter and line to house

Due Dates For

Homeowners insurance
Termite control
Garbage collection
Recycle collection

Telephone Numbers, Posted

Electric company	Police
Gas company	Ambulance
Water company	Road conditions
Cable company	Automobile tow service

Summary Statement: My concerned oldest son gave me the *Reader's Digest Repair Manual: The Complete Guide to Home Maintenance.* I have started a Service/Repair file of recommended persons. My coping philosophy is "If I can't fix it, they can." Between my own "bandaged thumb" efforts and the persons on my list, I should be able to manage.

MS. OR MR. FIX-IT

I'm a Lone Homeowner

My Lists for the Bare Basics

Summary Statement:

NEW FRIENDS

For My Personal Support Group

It just happened, the special combination of three friends I've made in this first year. All are widows. Peggy's husband died two months before mine. Edith has been a widow for about two years. And Betty has passed the four-year mark.

RECENT LOSS. Peggy really does understand where I am, any day. No matter what depression or catastrophe hits, I can call this friend. She listens and knows what I am experiencing. We can spend time together, sharing or choosing not to share. We take turns crying, or cry together. There is total acceptance. It's important she is there.

TWO-YEAR-AGO LOSS. I look at Edith and think, "She's come a long way; I'll be able to do this, too." Then I hear her say, "I still can't listen to the songs that were our favorites." Remarks like this help me face the reality that my own grief process will take more than the promised one year. She still remembers much of what I'm going through but doesn't need to sink to where I am. She remains stable and up. It feels good to be with her.

OVER FOUR-YEAR-AGO LOSS. Betty talks about her husband only as part of her life history. She is so assertive and independent. I am learning much from her. We have enjoyed some trips together. Somehow knowing I can talk about my grief with her frees me from having to do so. I can safely try on my "new self without Joe" with her.

The "How" of Making These New Friends

GROUP. After several sessions of being with Peggy in our Hospice Bereavement Group, I knew that we would have much in common. A lunch date gave us the opportunity to prove that this was true.

FRIENDS. Edith was a friend of friends of ours. Even though she did not know us personally, Edith attended Joe's Memorial Service. This act of caring drew me to her and we began doing things together.

TRAVEL. A travel agent put Betty and me together for a weekend trip we had individually chosen. We enjoyed being roommates and have attended an Elderhostel program together. Our times together are activity oriented.

Summary Statement: I realize how vital it is to have friends who understand how I feel. Their being at different stages in their loss gives me perspective in my grieving process. These friends are very precious and I will keep our friendships alive. . . . I'd like to think, however, that the next new friends I make will not be widows.

NEW FRIENDS

For My Personal Support Group

**My Support Group Friends and
What They Mean to Me**

Ways to Make New Friends

Summary Statement:

LONELINESS IS TO BE FELT

Alone Time Made Better

Friends ask, "What hurts the most?" Always I answer, "Loneliness for Joe. It never goes away." I don't want to run from this loneliness because I know to feel it is an important part of the grieving process. . . . But, my alone time can be enriched.

Feeling My Loneliness

Don't fight it; let the feelings come. Express aloud, on paper, physically (without hurting myself), and with tears.

When feelings of loneliness for him are blocked, do something to bring on the grief: look at pictures of him and us together, read some of his cards or letters, think about the ways I miss him, or find and hold something special that belonged to him.

Talk with others who loved him too. Cry together.

Structure my loneliness by containing it within a reasonable period of time. Then do something different. I call this "containment."

Making Alone Time Better

Create a lovely "alone place" in my home and schedule meditation time every day. Sit for twenty minutes, completely relaxed. Say one word over and over, like "peace," "love," "one." Ignore other thoughts. Let go completely. At the end of twenty minutes, come back slowly.

Determine the time of the week that I mind being alone the most (Sundays for me). List things I might do: sit at a different place in church; take turns, with alone friends, cooking and serving dinner; check television listing for special programs; drive to an area park and explore or sit and read; visit a museum; bake cookies with a borrowed kid; find a volunteer job for every Sunday.

Learn to treasure my time alone. Make a date with myself, dress up, fix a nice meal, serve it with music and candlelight. Give positive messages to myself. Stay dressed up for the rest of the evening . The next time a friend cannot go with me to something I want to attend, go alone. Consciously enjoy the moment.

Summary Statement: I need to differentiate between my loneliness for Joe and aloneness. Only then can I express my lonely-for-him feelings and make my alone periods more fulfilling. There are times when I now choose to be alone. In so doing, I value my own company and increase my feelings of self-worth.

LONELINESS IS TO BE FELT

Alone Time Made Better

Feeling My Loneliness

Making Alone Time Better

Summary Statement:

I'LL BE SEEING YOU

But Know You Are Not There

The man coming toward me on the street looked like Joe. I stood staring, my breath coming in little gasps. He was tall and thin. He even walked like Joe. He passed me at the corner. It certainly was not my husband. The tears came. What I wouldn't give to see Joe walking toward me again!

Joe, I Remember You

Coming up the steps to the deck with an armload of firewood.

Bending over the saw in your workshop.

Sitting in your chair, hands held together, fingertips touching, thinking.

Pouring batter on the griddle and flipping the pancakes.

Driving the tractor through the woods, on the trails you made.

Sitting on the deck at sunset, looking out over the valley.

Driving the car, seat back as far as it would go.

Reading the current news magazine in bed.

Pretending you were still asleep when it was time to get up.

Putting papers in the neatly organized files in your office.

Sitting across from me at the table, reaching for my hands to hold during our grace.

Cutting the loaf of bread in our favorite restaurant.

Sitting in church, next to me, at the end of "our" pew.

Walking the streets of the cities we visited, map in hand.

Watching the squirrel raiding the bird feeder and outsmarting him, one more time.

Summary Statement: It hurts to remember you in these places, and yet it is a "good" hurt. So I will continue to remember.

I'LL BE SEEING YOU

But Know You Are Not There

When I thought that I saw You:

I Remember You

Summary Statement:

HE WASN'T PERFECT

No One Is

It is difficult for me to recall things I did not like about Joe. He was so easy to live with. But, as in every relationship, there were times when we did not agree or behaviors of his bothered me. There is a tendency when a person dies to forget the negatives and only remember his attributes. Joe was human and I choose to remember him that way.

I Wish He

Had cared more about his appearance.

Did not overreact when I asked him to do something.

Had been more sociable.

Had been freer to express negative emotions.

Could have dealt with his fear of not having sufficient savings.

Had expressed a stronger faith in God.

Summary Statement: I did love him, just the way he was. But seeing him as he was makes grieving and letting go more possible.

For You the Reader

There is no way I can title an exercise in this area to fit your individual situation. The range goes from "He/she was a saint" all the way to "I'm glad he's/she's dead!" Many of us need help in working through deep anger and resentments toward the person who has died. That is beyond the scope of this book, and I trust you to get help if you need it. . . . Whatever you do, don't skip this exercise. Choose one of the titles on the next page that best fits you, or make up one of your own. Doing the exercise will help you to determine if you can work on this by yourself or with a friend, or if you need professional help. Resentments held in and buried can later cause a lot of trouble.

MY MATE WASN'T PERFECT

No One Is

Use one of the following (or develop your own): "I Wish He/She," "Why Couldn't He/She," "He/She Made My Life Difficult By," "I Hated It When He/She," "I'm **Really** Angry About," "I Hated Him/Her For."

Summary Statement:

I AFFIRM MYSELF

Again and Again

Many times in the past, I have written affirmations for myself, putting each one on the back of a business card. Where are they? Never mind. It is better that I make new ones which affirm where I am now. I remember that affirmations are strong and positive statements about who I am, my beliefs, strengths, and capabilities, and about how I expect to be treated. They need to be as short as possible.

My Affirmations

I, Marta, am a person of worth.
I, Marta, am unique.
I, Marta, have inner strength.
I, Marta, can cry and still be strong.
I, Marta, am a survivor.
I, Marta, value my health.
I, Marta, deserve to have my needs met.
I, Marta, have the capacity for change.
I, Marta, reach out to others.
I, Marta, have hope for the future.

Ways of Using My Affirmations

Put each one on a separate card. Carry them in my purse to read when I have to wait somewhere.

Choose one each day to put where I can see it while I eat.

Type or write each one ten times.

Put single ones in strategic places around the house: on mirrors, in often-opened drawers, on the microwave door, on the stove hood, etc.

Record them and then listen to the tape in the car.

Ask a friend to read them to me, prefacing each with "You, Marta."

Sit in a relaxed position and visualize myself being the way my affirmation says I am. Visualize each affirmation in this manner.

Summary Statement: I will read and experience these affirmations until they are part of me. I will call them to mind throughout the day. Their truths will enable me to stand tall with my head held high. I will add more and continue to visualize each.

I AFFIRM MYSELF

Again and Again

My Affirmations

Ways of Using My Affirmations

Summary Statement:

I CARE ABOUT MY FAMILY

So I Put My House in Order

With inherited longevity and good health in his favor, I expected Joe to live to be one hundred! In accepting the reality of his death, it makes me realize that I too am mortal.

Things to Get Done

Update my will, to be in effect until I make a Living Trust.

Make an appointment with my lawyer and have him prepare:
Durable Power of Attorney
Living Will
Living Trust (will replace will and avoid probate)

Make a list of my material possessions designated for certain persons.

Prepare a statement of burial wishes and suggestions for a Memorial Service.

Write a loving letter to each of my sons, for them to read after my death.

Put all of the above in one of two places:

Safety deposit box. Get an extra key and signature signing privilege for my son.

Fire safety file. It is also to hold canceled checks and income tax returns for at least the three previous years.

Type a list entitled "What My Family Should Know"; send copies to my sons. Include names, addresses, and phone numbers of my lawyer, minister, insurance companies, broker, CPA, etc. Also include a list of important papers and where they can be found.

Summary Statement: Much as I dislike having to do these things, I believe each is important and needs to be done soon. I will keep this list in full sight on my desk and check off each task when completed.

I CARE ABOUT MY FAMILY

So I Put My House in Order

Things to Get Done

Summary Statement:

PUT THE CHERRY BACK ON TOP!

And Other Things for Me

After months of not bothering to eat grapefruit, I sat down at breakfast with half of one in front of me. Something was missing—the cherry on the top. Always for Joe and me, I had drizzled the halves with honey and topped them with a cherry. Am I not worth a cherry on the top? What other things am I not doing that I did before and I still deserve?

I Deserve To

Comb my hair and put on lipstick first thing in the day.

Start making my bed again.

Make brewed coffee to start my day, instead of instant.

Go for a drive on a pretty day. Discover a new restaurant or store.

Make pancakes, just for me.

Give myself nice presents at Christmas, Valentine's Day, and my birthday.

Look for a new recipe, fix it for me, and freeze leftovers in individual portions.

Make dinner alone special. Freshen my makeup. Change clothes for my TV dinner date with my favorite news commentator.

Buy a new article of clothing in a bright color.

Treat myself to a manicure or pedicure.

Take myself out to eat at a nice restaurant. Read a book or "people watch."

Program a relaxing bath: bubbles, music, candlelight.

Summary Statement: I am special and I deserve any of these things I choose to do for me. I will look for more special treats.

PUT THE CHERRY BACK ON TOP!

And Other Things for Me

When and how have I been denying that I am special?

I Deserve To

Summary Statement:

THAT MAGIC MOMENT

The Story of How We Met

Tiny incidents of that evening are etched upon my memory. I know what I was wearing, black slacks and a tapestry jacket. The jacket still hangs in the back of my closet, having been in and out of style many times. I like to recall that time.

One enchanted evening, I did meet a stranger across a crowded room. The setting was a birthday party for my best friend. Most of the people I knew. . . but, who was that tall man across the room? He was eating peanuts like he had just discovered them! At that moment he glanced up and our eyes met and held. When I could disentangle myself from the group I was with, I made my way to where he stood. He didn't say hello but simply offered me peanuts! Little did I know that he would always share what he enjoyed with me, for the rest of our lives together!

We didn't begin with chit-chat as most people do, but at a deeper level: our relationship with our grown children, the world situation, and many other things. Finally, we got around to "I'm Joe" and "I'm Marta."

The friends I had come with were leaving early to go to another party. What stroke of fate kept me from going with them? "I'll stay and take a taxi home," I said.

Later, Joe and I found ourselves together again. This time it felt like we were old friends, and we picked up where we had left off. We had so much to say to each other. When he asked me to go to dinner with him, I agreed with no hesitation. At this time in my life such a response was totally out of character. I learned later that Joe's even being at the party was unusual for him.

As we walked to the place where I could catch a taxi, he lightly put his arm about my shoulder and helped me around some obstacles. My eyes filled with tears, remembering some past hurts. In that moment I knew that here was a man who would protect and help me, and my intuition proved true.

Summary Statement: It feels so good to relive that evening. I am so thankful that, against so many odds, we did meet. We sensed that there could be something special between us, and we made it happen!

THAT MAGIC MOMENT

The Story of How We Met

Summary Statement:

THE GUILT TRIP GOES ON

Unless I End It

I've heard myself saying, "One thing I'm thankful for is that I have no regrets." That isn't entirely true. When I look deep enough, I find those guilty feelings that were there all the time.

I Feel Guilty About	Ending It
Not fulfilling the one request he made in the hospital.	Hear him saying (if he could), "Marta, it's OK." Accept it.
Not talking with him about his death when it became inevitable.	Somehow I felt that talking about it would make it real, and I could not deal with that. Understand; forgive myself.
Spending so much of our time together talking about my needs and activities.	He was the silent type. Acknowledge only the guilt I'm due; let that amount go.
Planning so many trips the year before he became ill. There were jobs he wanted to do at home.	He enjoyed our trips. Let myself mourn his unfulfilled dreams.
Giving him gifts I wanted him to have and so few that I knew he wanted.	You're only human. Forgive your failings. Remember the gifts he loved.
Taking personally our big discussion about finances. He got upset and I struck back.	I now understand why we each reacted as we did. I forgive myself for the way I handled my part.

Summary Statement: In these situations guilt serves no purpose. It gets me stuck in my grieving process. I need to recognize guilt, check its validity, forgive where needed, and be sure I let it go.

THE GUILT TRIP GOES ON

Unless I End It

I Feel Guilty About   **Ending It**

Summary Statement:

WHO TAKES CARE OF ME?

I Do

Loss of a spouse puts me at the **very top** of the Stress Factor List. What if I get sick? There's no one to say, "Let me tuck you in bed and bring you some chicken soup." I feel physically, mentally, and emotionally drained. That scares me. I'm a prime target for a health hazard. If ever I needed to observe basic health care, it is NOW.

Every Day I Promise Myself That I Will

KEEP TO A REGULAR SLEEP SCHEDULE, whether I sleep solidly or not. I will limit medication to early weeks of the grieving period.

EXERCISE, doing something I enjoy. Include a friend whenever I can.

EAT RIGHT, which means lots of fruits, vegetables (raw is fine), whole grains in bread and cereal. Stick to nonfat or low-fat dairy products. Avoid alcohol and caffeine in any form.

EXPRESS FEELINGS through crying, journal writing, talking with family and friends, or physical outlets.

NURTURE MYSELF with loving and caring messages all through the day. Watch out for put-downs and negatives. "Tape" positives on top.

MEDITATE/PRAY, working toward ten to twenty minutes twice a day. Consider relaxation, watch breathing, and repeat a favorite word technique.

Later I Promise Myself To

Tailor a stress release program to my needs.

Keep a "Talk to Doctor" file. Include notes and articles to share.

Expand my exercise program. Include variety, especially a weight-bearing exercise.

Be aware of eating to fill the void or not eating, being lonely.

Establish new eating places and patterns.

Take vitamin, mineral, and calcium supplements if needed, no megadoses. Take Vitamin B6, the "stress vitamin," this first year.

Check my weight once a week. Keep within the recommended range with a healthy eating program and exercise.

Drink six to eight glasses of water per day. Keep a filled water pitcher on the counter as a reminder.

Find a buddy to remind each other of monthly breast self-examinations.

Put reminders of appointments on a calendar: dental, eye exam, physical, mammogram, etc.

Be careful of steps, slippery areas (shower, tub), kitchen knives.

Read *Prevention* or *Health* magazine.

Find a volunteer job that makes me feel fulfilled.

Cultivate healthy-minded friends. Compare notes; share what's new.

Summary Statement: I will make a "Have you . . ." card with the six areas listed. This goes where I can see it as a daily reminder. Later I will work on the longer list, checking off as I go. Taking care of my health is the most important thing I can do for myself.

WHO TAKES CARE OF ME?
I Do

Every Day I Promise Myself That I Will

Later I Promise Myself To

Summary Statement:

DEAR JOE, IT'S ME, MARTA

Letters Not to Be Mailed

Joe had made a small request while he was in the hospital that I did not fulfill. After he died, I recalled this incident. For days I wallowed in remorse that I had not done what he had asked. It was as if I needed something to feel guilty about. Nothing I did made me feel any better. In desperation I grabbed my legal pad and started writing a letter to him, pouring out my heart. After pages of "talking" to him, I felt relief. Many letters have been written since then, prefaced with "I know you're not going to get this, but I need to talk to you."

Excerpts from My Letters to Joe

. . . I'm so thankful you don't know about the family problems. You'd be hurting, too. But here I can tell you. . . . Is it possible that, wherever you are, you are aware of only the good things happening to me? I believe that is true. I also see you being healthy and happy.

. . . Edith and I saw *Nunsense* today at the dinner theater where you and I used to go. I haven't laughed that hard since you've been gone. It was such a release! . . . Now I'm having different feelings. I feel guilty that I had so much fun without you. I didn't even think about you during the play. Isn't it silly for me to feel that way? You, of all people, would want me to enjoy life. I hope I can remember that.

. . . I'm so frustrated and upset! The carpenter was here today. The questions are endless! What had you planned to do with . . . ? Where did you put . . . ? What should I do in this situation . . . ? And that? Where do I get . . . ? If you were here you would know the answers. As I write this I realize why I'm resenting Jim's presence so intensely. He represents your dying and not being able to do these things, and my inadequacies. How can I blame you for dying? So I'm blaming Jim and myself. Now I understand.

. . . You will find it hard to believe this. I'm taking a wood carving class! It's the last thing you would expect me to do. You'd love it and do a super job. Is that why I enrolled? Tonight was the first class and I cut my thumb. You know how great I am with tools! But you can tell my mouse is a mouse!

. . . Sometimes I've looked forward to today, the year anniversary of your death. When the going was rough this year, I'd say to myself what I had heard so many times, "The first year is the hardest." So here I am on January 25, and it still hurts! It's not over. But I have survived. I've let myself grieve and I've taken control of my life. Those were my only goals this year. I can hear you say, "You've done well, kid. I'm proud of you." I feel proud of me, too.

Summary Statement: My letters to Joe provide a special kind of release. There are also times when reading them again is just what I need to do.

Letter Not to Be Mailed

Date_________________

Dear_______________________, It's me, ______________________

Summary Statement:

MAKE MY HOME MINE

I'm the One Who Must Live Here

It is in the bedroom where I miss Joe the most. If I make some changes, especially in the area I can see from the bed, maybe it will be easier to be there.

Situation	Plan for Change
Bedroom with most of the furnishings built in.	Put bench along wall. Add artificial tree.
No seating in kitchen. I refuse to face his empty chair in the dining area.	Get bar stools and eat at island in kitchen. Look out window.
His office in the house, with no one using it.	Donate his books. Empty desk drawers. Adapt his files for me.
His garage work area in disarray .	Put Joe's special tools out of sight. Organize what I expect to use.
Bird feeder a delight, but requires daily refilling.	Purchase a bird feeder with much larger capacity.
Steps to deck often icy in winter.	Construct readily accessible wood storage unit just outside door.
Poor lighting where I've chosen to sit in living room.	Find lamp that will furnish adequate lighting.

Summary Statement: Nothing will bring him back, but I have a life to live. I need not feel guilty, as I was doing, about making changes. It is with pride that I work within my home to make it more live-able and enjoyable for me.

MAKE MY HOME MINE

I'm the One Who Must Live Here

Feelings I have about making changes in my home:

Situation   Plan For Change

Summary Statement:

LOOKING GOOD

Putting My Best Face Forward

For a long period of time after Joe's death, I did not care how I looked. It was a matter of survival, one day at a time. Before, I had enjoyed making myself attractive, mostly for me. What about now?

Ideas for Improving My Appearance

Get a new hairstyle, with regular trims. Consider highlighting or coloring.

Have a makeover done at a department store. Will get ideas and don't have to buy.

Take to Salvation Army my drab, dull clothes that do nothing for me. Buy a few clothes in happy colors that light me up. Include one for special occasions.

Sew stylish new buttons on tired but still good old jacket. Resurrect other pieces of clothing.

Treat myself to a manicure and new polish.

Sample perfume sprays and select one that fits me.

Make a pact with a friend, who also needs to lose weight, and get rid of these ten extra pounds.

Replace my worn out exercise clothes with an attractive new outfit.

Choose a new pair of earrings in a style I've never worn before.

Tilt the car mirror up slightly, forcing me to sit tall.

Summary Statement: My self-worth is not to be measured by my appearance. As I am feeling better on the inside, however, I want my appearance to match that. I choose to become more attractive. This is a neat list of fun things to do.

LOOKING GOOD

Putting My Best Face Forward

How I Feel about How I Look:

Ideas for Improving My Appearance

Summary Statement:

A DECISION I NEED TO MAKE

Keep Francis; Let Francis Go

Five weeks after Joe's death, my car was totaled. Thankfully, no one was seriously injured. So I have been driving Francis, our second car, full time. Francis is a '67 Dynamic Olds 88 we purchased for three hundred dollars six years ago. We fell in love with Francis and had him put in mint condition. She was Frances when Joe drove her and Francis when I was behind the wheel. He performed beautifully on two long trips. BUT, I don't need two cars. Should I get rid of Francis and purchase a new car? I choke up at the thought!

Pro (Keep Francis)	Con (Let Francis Go)
Heavy car; I feel safer	Guzzles gas; low gas mileage
Insurance cost is low	Doesn't have front wheel drive
Low maintenance and upkeep	Heater doesn't work up to par
White is a "safe" color	Requires large parking space
Excellent mechanic available	Need big area to turn around
Great mechanical shape	AM radio only
Huge trunk for hauling	
Beautiful, long classic lines	
Solid ride; holds the road	
Body in great shape; no rust or rattles	
Paid for; no car payments	
Probably safe from car hijackers	
Great sentimental attachment	

Summary Statement: After listing the above, I have decided that Francis will live, at least for now. I will have an FM radio and cassette player installed and ride in style! This pro and con decision-making process I can use for other decisions.

Other Decisions Ahead of Me

Stay in this home or move to a smaller one.
Remain in this area or move closer to my family.
Go back to school, or not.
Find a job or do volunteer work.
Stay in my chosen field or try something new.
Take a trip next year.
Get professional help with investments or do it on my own.

PRO AND CON DECISION MAKING PROCESS

Description of a decision I need to make and why:

Pro   Con

Other Decisions Ahead of Me

Summary Statement:

MEMORIALS

For Memory and Tributes

I want to remember Joe, the life and love we shared. I also will create memorials as tributes to the life he lived.

Memorials to Joe	Their Meaning for Me
Plant a pink dogwood tree where I can see it from the kitchen. It will bloom in the early spring.	Spring was his favorite season. Pink dogwood is special to me, as he was.
Have a heart made from his wedding band. Wear it on a chain under my clothes.	His heart will be next to mine, where I can feel it all the time.
Donate books to the library in his memory.	He loved to read, for education and for fun.
Sort through our photos. Make albums of his life and our time together.	He lived a full and happy life. Here is the proof.
Volunteer to help serve food on Thanksgiving and Christmas at the Salvation Army.	The Salvation Army was Joe's favorite charity.
Contribute to a scholarship fund in his name.	Young people will receive help to go forward with their lives.

Summary Statement: As I pay tribute to him, through memorials I choose, I feel closer to him, and his life continues.

MEMORIALS
For Memory and Tributes

Memorials to ______________   **Their Meaning for Me**

Summary Statement:

A BREAK IN THE CLOUDS

That I Create

In that fuzzy time, when my eyes were still shut but I knew that it was morning, I realized that I did not want to open my eyes and face the day. How much easier it would be just to drift back to sleep and pretend IT never happened. No. TODAY I will create a little happiness for myself.

Something to Look Forward To

Tie a yellow ribbon on a pretty basket. Fill it with cards and letters that offer comfort. Read and reread them as needed throughout the day.

Memorize an inspirational quote, such as a Bible verse, and repeat it to myself all through the day.

Put on rain gear and walk with the light rain on my face.

Gather flowers and place them in small containers around the house.

Call one of my best friends for no reason except to be in touch.

Simmer whole cloves and cinnamon in a saucepan. Let the memories come: mother's apple pie, special Christmas cookies, and red hot candies.

Have music tapes ready for periods of cleaning, mealtime, and relaxing.

Make a small purchase, maybe a magazine or scented candle. Use it as a reward for getting some thing difficult finished.

Sit with a travel brochure and dream about taking a trip.

Select a book or audiocassette book at the library.

Discover a new flavored coffee or herb tea.

Find a seed catalog and pick out bulbs to plant in the spring.

Send a picture postcard of my area to invite a friend for a visit.

Rent a light video and have popcorn ready to munch while I watch it.

Select an exotic fruit and plan when to have it as a treat.

Send a tiny, secret gift to someone I love.

Make a luncheon date for a day soon and put it on my calendar.

Celebrate the first leaf to fall in autumn, the first snowflake of winter, and bring in a small branch with buds in the early spring.

Summary Statement: Small treats can help make long days bearable. I will plan something special every day, look forward to it, savor it, and gain strength for facing the rest of the day.

A BREAK IN THE CLOUDS

That I Create

Something to Look Forward To

Summary Statement:

MY MEMORY QUILT

It Keeps Me Warm

Summary Statement: I snuggle under this quilt and feel loved and secure. It is always here where I can touch the feelings I had then and smile, remembering Joe and our years together.

MY MEMORY QUILT

It Keeps Me Warm

Summary Statement:

THAT CAN'T BE ME

That Person Is Old!

Recently I was leafing through my son's photo album. Seeing a picture of an older woman I did not recognize, I asked, "Who is that?" He replied, "Why, Mom, that's you." It had been taken after Joe's death. There was no denying, the woman in that photo was haggard and looked old. I feel I have lost a youthful part of me, and I understand why. I'd like to bring it back.

I've Lost	How to Regain
Stamina	Begin by walking three times a week. Use stationary bike on other days or when it rains. Try yoga tape. Work toward a balanced combination.
My excitement over little things	Focus on at least one beautiful thing each day. Really taste every morsel of a favorite food, like a slice of bread.
The bounce in my step	Wear a rubber band on my wrist as a reminder to walk with a purpose.
My smile	Encourage myself to smile at everyone I meet.
Good posture (walking and sitting tall)	Do mental and mirror checks throughout the day.
Laughter	Start reading the comics. Collect jokes to share with friends. Read books by Erma Bombeck, George Burns, and other humorists. Look at funny videos and TV shows.
A reason for living	Make list of short term and long term goals. Outline some plans. Share with a partner; inspire each other.

Summary Statement: I'm on my way. Each little step helps, onward and upward.

IS THAT PERSON ME?

How old do I feel? If someone took a picture of me or I looked in a mirror, how old would I say that person was? Is that older than I really am?

I've Lost   How to Regain

Summary Statement:

I NEED TO GO BACK

To Where It Happened

I sat in the car, unable to put my hand on the door handle to open it. Joe's nephew said, "You don't have to go in; you can change your mind." But I knew I had to go into the Houston hospital where Joe had died. The five weeks spent there had been so terrible that I had blocked them from my mind. I needed to make that experience real before I could let it go.

Where I Need to Go and

What I Need to Do

HOSPITAL WHERE HE DIED. Walk the hall to "our" room. Go in if I can. Relive the experience. Say my good-byes to Joe again. Make my circuit walk around the halls. Visit the chapel and pray. Talk to the nurses who were there when we were. Go out the front door and leave his "dying time" behind.

OUR FIRST HOME. Walk along the street. Take pictures. Sit on a bench and remember. Go to our church. Visit the library. Spend time with our favorite neighbor who still lives next door. Walk the aisles in our supermarket. Eat at the corner restaurant. Remember, treasure, and give to the past.

WHERE WE LIVED MOST OF OUR MARRIED LIFE. Call a friend in that area and make arrangements to stay with her. Set a luncheon date and invite all the friends who still live there. Talk about Joe and the times we spent together. Take the same early morning walk we always took. Visit his work place and mine. Eat at the very special restaurant we always called "ours." Drink a toast to Joe. Devote one day to making a video of our life there. Take with me when I leave what I want to remember, always conscious that it belongs to yesterday.

Summary Statement: These pilgrimages are so painful, but necessary. I trust myself that in each place I will know what I need to do. I will allow plenty of time to recall, to feel, to grieve, and then to let go. In letting go of the past, I make room for the future.

I NEED TO GO BACK
To Where It Happened

Where I Need to Go and

What I Need to Do

Summary Statement:

I BELIEVE IN ME

My Positive Traits Are Still There

"You are so well organized," everyone used to tell me. Admittedly, that was true. If ever there was a time when I needed to bring structure into my life, it is now. I would feel more secure and in control. Also, I must have other attributes that I can rely on now.

Positive Attributes I Can Think Of

friendly	cheerful	curious
<u>organized</u>	attractive	outgoing
humorous	caring	serene
resourceful	thoughtful	healthy
determined	<u>creative</u>	sympathetic
worthwhile	<u>understanding</u>	capable
hardworking	independent	giving
gentle	sincere	aesthetic
quiet	dependable	<u>forgiving</u>
courageous	optimistic	contented
confident	tenacious	assertive
intelligent	vivacious	cooperative
tolerant	<u>motivated</u>	kind
insightful	helpful	resilient
tender	religious	honest
realistic	open	honorable
courageous	worthwhile	humble

I will underline characteristics that I have and copy on a card:

I AM

ORGANIZED
CREATIVE
UNDERSTANDING
MOTIVATED
FORGIVING

Summary Statement: As I look at my card each day, I will think of ways to use these strengths. I will visualize myself being that way.

I BELIEVE IN ME

My Positive Traits Are Still There

My Positive Traits   How I Can Use Them Now

Summary Statement:

PUT TO GOOD USE

When I Am Ready

In the beginning, if I started to move Joe's things, I felt like I was getting rid of him. Slowly, I was able to pack away some items making more room for mine. They went into drawers and an empty closet. "I'll take care of them some day." For me, that day is here.

Items	Possible Use
Blood pressure machine	*Donate it to the Medical Clinic.
His work coat	Wear it myself when I carry in wood and fill the bird feeders.
Technical books	*Donate them to the University.
Mustache trimming set	Offer it to son who has a mustache.
Pocket knife, from Bangkok	Give it to son who especially loved to hear about Joe's travels.
Several pairs of eyeglasses	Donate them at Eye Clinic.
Favorite red suede vest	Have it altered to fit me.
Carpentry tools	Give them to son who is remodeling home.
London Fog raincoat	Give it to Joe's nephew who wears same size.
Magazines	Drop them off at library.
Leftover clothes	*Donate them to Salvation Army.
Tiny pocket comb he always carried	Keep it in the bottom of my purse, where I can touch it at any time.
Electric razor	Offer it to son who gave it to him.
The rest of his personal things which I want to keep	Place them lovingly in cedar chest. Look at them whenever I choose.

*Obtain donation statement for income tax.

Summary Statement: For me it has been helpful to wait to disperse Joe's belongings. I can make wiser decisions now and choose people who will appreciate items of his. His memory lives on in the things he used.

PUT TO GOOD USE

When I Am Ready

My situation in dealing with my mate's belongings:

       Remaining Items   **Possible Use**

Summary Statement:

TO BE LIKE JOE

I'm Free to Choose

Joe had offered to make a file cabinet for me, indicating that he would begin that day. After seeing him sitting in his favorite chair for a long time and seemingly doing nothing, I asked, "What happened to the file project?" "I'm working on it," he replied.

Lessons I Learned from Joe

Thinking and planning time are as important as working time.

Don't sweat the little things.
Most problems are just that.
Save your time and energy for the big ones.

Travel, to be appreciated fully, must be done leisurely.
Adventure on foot whenever possible.

Select one task at a time.
Follow it through to completion and do it well.

Accept people as they are.
They are doing the best they can, for now.

Also accept yourself.
Forgive your mistakes.
Savor your successes.

Summary Statement: These were Joe's words of wisdom that he lived by and that I admire. I choose to make them part of my life. In so doing, Joe's principles live on.

TO BE LIKE__________

I'm Free to Choose

Lessons I Learned from_____________

That I Choose for Myself

Summary Statement:

SO LET US CELEBRATE!

I Count My Blessings

Every Sunday morning our minister starts the service with an introductory phrase followed by, "So let us celebrate!" During the week, when there was something for which Joe was thankful, he would often say, "So let us celebrate," mimicking the minister's voice and intonations exactly. It always made me smile. I realize I have not been celebrating my blessings.

I Celebrate My

Family who loves me

Two best friends, and other friends

"Talking" relationship with God

Church and worship that spiritually fulfill me

Five senses in good working order

Home where I feel secure

Returning appetite and good health

Project which gives purpose to my life

Trusted renter in my apartment

Finances sufficient for my needs

Treasured memories of my time with Joe

Beginnings of a new life

Summary Statement: My many blessings have gotten drowned in my sorrows. Here I lift them out, one by one. I will list more. I need to read this list often and realize how truly blessed I am.

SO LET US CELEBRATE!

I Count My Blessings

Summary Statement:

TIME GOES BY

Nothing Gets Done

In the early months after Joe's death, I was neither aware of nor cared if things piled up to be done. I doubt if I saw them. Grieving was all-consuming. Now, however, my productive nature is beginning to surface. I am increasingly frustrated as the days float by and nothing seems to be accomplished. What happens to my time?

Time Wasters	Time Savers
Reading newspapers, catalogs, and junk mail	Use TV or mealtime to skim these.
Jumping from one task to another	Train myself to finish one task before starting another.
Moving in slow motion	Set small reward on completion of task. Enjoy.
Allowing phone calls to take too much time	Consolidate calls. Stick to topic. Do body exercises.
Putting off jobs I don't like, letting them pile up	Make list for the day, put in rank order, check off list.
Spending hours watching news and reading news magazines	Use TV and radio news time to get other things done. Skim magazines.
Making numerous trips into town, taking longer than expected	Keep running list of errands to do in one trip.
Looking at the total list of everything that needs to be done and giving up in despair	Take one day at a time. At end of day take pride in finished tasks. Begin with new plan the next day.

Summary Statement: These are better ways of making use of my time. I'll work while I work, play when I play, and find both fulfilling.

TIME GOES BY

Nothing Gets Done

My Time Management Assessment:

Time Wasters   Time Savers

Summary Statement:

THE THREE LETTER WORD
What About Sex?

I am a sexual being. Why is there no exercise in my spiral notebooks designed to deal with sex? Because when Joe died I chose to push it aside and pretend that part of me did not exist. That is not fair to me. Nor is it being true to our beautiful sexual relationship. I did not die when Joe did. But what can I do?

STOP RUNNING. Don't look away when there are tender love scenes on TV or in movies. Watch and let myself feel, even if it hurts terribly. Read, instead of skipping over, those intimate parts in books. Bring back into focus couples holding hands and smiling at each other. Let myself see men as men again.

KEEP ALIVE PHYSICALLY. I had no qualms about pleasuring myself during long absences from Joe or when health prevented sexual intercourse. The first time I tried after his death, however, I couldn't continue. I curled up in a ball and sobbed, missing him and the sexual fulfillment we knew. To keep juices flowing and prevent atrophy of my sexual being, I need to continue this avenue of release.

FEEL SEXUAL. Sexuality in the broader sense means I can feel like a woman without a sexual partner. I choose to look attractive and move in graceful ways, not as a come-on for men, but as a reflection of the real me. I **am** a woman.

BE WILLING TO RISK. There may be a close relationship in my future. Up to now I've rejected it, saying I don't want it. I am becoming a whole person. I am free to choose. There is no need to rush to fill the void or sublimate what is lost. I can take my time and move from friendship to respect and then to trust, if it is right for me. A new relationship will be different from what I have known. If it is not to be, I can handle that, too.

Summary Statement: Becoming more sexually alive is being true to myself and to my love life with Joe. I will "tend" this part of me. I remain open to experiencing new intimacies, while keeping the woman in me alive.

THE THREE LETTER WORD

What About Sex?

Where Am I Sexually?

What Do I Need to Do

Summary Statement:

IT WAS A COMFORT

When They Reached Out

I remember with such affection the loving things some people did and said. I continue to feel loved, just remembering.

Listening

In the beginning my greatest need was just to talk. It helped when I felt certain people really wanted to hear what I needed to say. I saw acceptance in their eyes. They did not interrupt and seemed comfortable when I said nothing or just cried. They held my hand. No advice was given. They listened as long as I needed to talk.

Words

"It's OK. I'm still listening. I have lots of time." . . . "I always admired Joe. He was my mentor. Much of what he taught me has stayed with me." . . . "I remember the love in Joe's eyes when he talked about you." . . . "In all the many years I knew Joe, I never heard him say a critical word about another person." . . . "I don't know how you feel, but if you want to talk, I'll listen." . . . "I have been thinking about you and wanted to call and tell you that I care." . . . "I'm hurting, not like you, but I miss him, too." . . . "I'll just be here beside you." . . . "Let the tears come; I don't mind." . . . "I love you."

Deeds

A friend called long distance every evening at 9:30 for the first ten days I was alone. "I'm just calling to hear about your day and to tuck you into bed." . . . There were notes, even though short, that continued long after others stopped writing; food, in disposable pans, that could be frozen and used later; a specific invitation to lunch or dinner. . . . A visitor brought a box of new herbal tea. . . . "I'm going grocery shopping. Want to come along?" . . . A Peace plant was sent to my home with a loving note. . . . A touch on the arm, hand squeeze, or a full-fledged hug were given naturally and sincerely. . . . "Let's plan to spend the day together on your anniversary. I'll think of things for us to do." . . . Letters and calls were received long after his death.

Summary Statement: As I write the above, I remember how good each contact felt and the comfort it brought. With these in mind, I can choose more wisely what to do for others when they are hurting.

IT WAS A COMFORT
When They Reached Out

Listening

Words

Deeds

Summary Statement:

WIDOWED, MARRIED, OR SINGLE

Where Am I Now?

The form had only two places to check:____ Married or _____ Single. There was no _____Widowed to hide behind. I hate that word anyway. So what am I, married or single? Or do I write in "widow"? I wrestle below.

WIDOW. That's not me. A widow is dressed in black, with a matching black veil. She walks slowly, alone, following the casket to the grave in the rain. She never smiles and talks constantly about her husband and cries as she does. How awful! How did I get that picture so fixed in my mind? No wonder I refuse to label myself "widow."

MARRIED. Legally, I am no longer married. But I can still write "Mrs." before my name and use his last name as mine. I wear the wedding band he gave me. Doesn't that make me married? I feel married. Am I clinging to the married state because I cannot face the reality of his death? That would make sense.

SINGLE. This sounds even worse! It brings to mind desperately lonely people reaching out to other lonely people in bars and singles' clubs. It could mean dating and all that. That's not for me.

Checking Out and

Moving between States

WIDOW. I never wear black; it's not my color. I now consciously choose bright colors that look good on me. I don't have to talk about Joe all the time. I still get tears in my eyes but not at every reminder of him. Often I write my name as Marta Felber and it looks OK. I've thought about a time ahead when I will take off my ring.

MARRIED. I want to feel married because that makes Joe seem closer. I don't want to lose him. The reality I must face is that he is dead. Our marriage in the here and now no longer exists. That hurts terribly, but I need to let it go. Ours was a good marriage, but it is over.

SINGLE. I can be single and not be looking for another relationship. I can begin to operate from the state of singleness with strength. This means I am my own person, unique. I do not have to depend on someone else for who I am. I am me.

Summary Statement: Except on legal forms, I am free to choose what I am. It's OK to see myself as either married, widowed, or single. I believe I am in transition, moving between these states, becoming an independent single. That's OK, too.

WIDOWED, MARRIED, OR SINGLE

Where Am I Now?

How I Feel about Being:

Widowed

Married

Single

Summary Statement:

THE YO-YO YEAR

It's Been Up and Down

What an appropriate image! A yo-yo goes up and down, down and up. That is exactly how my year has gone.

UP: Held up really well during his death and services.
  DOWN: Fell apart ten days later when everyone left.

DOWN: "I don't want to live without him," I said over and over.
  UP: "But I don't want to die, and I won't."

UP: Had a calm period for a couple of weeks.
  DOWN: Had six disasters within a few days.

UP: Appreciated my first trip away from home.
  DOWN: I was devastated on return; he wasn't there!

UP: Took a quick look at finances and decided I could manage.
  DOWN: I was hit with two huge expenditures I had not expected.

UP: There were promises of an easy and early estate settlement.
  DOWN: There were complications, with probate dragging on and on.

UP: Spent seven fulfilling days in San Francisco with a friend.
  DOWN: I was confined to bed with a sinus infection on return.

UP: Sang happy birthday to our two-year-old twin granddaughters.
  DOWN: Realized Joe won't see them grow up.

UP: Survived Christmas better than I thought I would.
  DOWN: Sunk to a deep depression on New Year's Day.

Summary Statement: This has been a rough year with many ups and downs. I feel good that I have survived as well as I have. Life will begin to level off. I am sure of that.

THE YO-YO YEAR
It's Been Up and Down

My Specific Yo-Yo Times

Summary Statement:

IT WILL GET BETTER

That's What Everyone Said

Everyone I talked to made this promise. In the beginning I resented hearing over and over, "It will get better." At that point I couldn't focus on the future, only on the tremendous pain of the present. Nearing the end of my first year of grieving, I realize that all those persons were right. It is getting better.

It's Getting Better - How I Know

I Compare NOW with BEFORE

NOW I don't cry as much as I did. . . . BEFORE, a song, sight, thought, ad, item in the grocery store would trigger tears.

NOW I dream about him less often. When I do, the dreams are about times we enjoyed. . . . BEFORE, the dreams were often of his illness and death.

NOW I don't feel I have to talk about him all the time. . . . BEFORE, I needed to tell everyone I met, "My husband died."

NOW I can think more clearly, focus on a problem, am less forgetful. . . . BEFORE, I was constantly confused, forgetting to do important things, driving to the wrong place, etc.

NOW my weight is almost normal. . . . BEFORE, I was underweight, then overweight.

NOW I'm sleeping through most nights. . . . BEFORE, I had trouble getting to sleep and then was waking at 2 or 4 A.M., unable to get back to sleep.

NOW I am reaching out to others in need. . . . BEFORE, I was totally submerged in my own loss.

NOW I can begin to think about goals, short term and long range. . . . BEFORE, I felt it didn't matter what happened to the rest of my life.

NOW I find myself laughing spontaneously. I'm smiling again. . . . BEFORE, every laugh was forced and I felt my face would crack.

Summary Statement: My days have gotten better and will continue to do so. I need to stop from time to time and acknowledge these positive changes. Then I can move in the direction of claiming my new life.

IT WILL GET BETTER

That's What Everyone Said

How I felt when people said, "It will get better:"

It Is Getting Better - How I Know

I Compare NOW with BEFORE

Summary Statement:

GOOD-BYES ARE HARD TO SAY

But the Time Has Come

Good-byes are necessary and even healthy. They provide closure and complete unfinished business. The time has come for me to remember and say good-bye to my life with Joe, our hopes and dreams.

I Need to Say Good-Bye To

Learning new things together: Computer literacy, "throwing" a pot, Elderhostel programs, acting workshops, courses at the University, lessons for South American dancing, or bird watching and identification of calls. I may do some of these things, but it is good-bye to our sharing these experiences.

Our "dates" taking each other out to eat. The one being taken did not know the destination, adding suspense. It was a neat thing to do and we did it for years. But it will be no more for us. Good-bye.

The best traveling companion I ever had. He taught me to "hang loose." Before I met him, I had to do every touristy thing. "If you run yourself ragged from morning to night, you won't remember a thing. You'll be exhausted," he claimed. "We'll choose a couple of things each day that we really want to see or do and then relax." How wise he was. Good-bye to my best traveling companion.

Using each other as sounding boards when we had concerns and problems related to family members. He was the only one who really understood. I say good-bye to my "special listener."

Growing old together. Somehow I did not dread those advancing years, knowing we would be in it together. I was confident that we would poke fun at our aches and pains, exercise together and eat healthy. Joe would have mellowed with age; he was that type. I let my "ageless" partner go.

The lover who shared my bed, his body that I could touch and feel, the many hugs and closeness. Good-bye to all those intimate times.

Summary Statement: The memories I can keep forever. I say good-bye to his actual presence. I let him go.

GOOD-BYES ARE HARD TO SAY
But the Time Has Come

I Need to Say Good-bye To

Summary Statement:

NEW YEAR'S DAY

Can Be Any Day

Last January 1 was a complete washout! I allowed a disturbing telephone conversation with a family member to push me into deep depression. Any thoughts of evaluating my past year and making resolutions were abandoned. . . . I've chosen TODAY instead as my New Year's Day. I take stock of my life.

WHERE HAVE I BEEN? I've been to the bottom! Those periods of deep mourning for Joe were the absolute pits. I went through it, as I knew I had to, but thank God the worst is over. I've dealt with frustrations, disappointments, and loneliness. I'm learning to talk to myself with more nurturing words. Nights were the hardest, but I survived. Joe's belongings have been shared or saved. Memorials have been established. I've made new friends. My affairs are more in order. Much of the guilt has been released. I am learning to take better care of myself. I have found strength to go on. I've come a long way.

WHERE AM I NOW? I'm not the same as I was before Joe died. I now am a person in my own right, not sharing an identity role with another. Without being selfish or totally self-centered, I place more value on myself. I am beginning to experience today as being more important than yesterday or tomorrow. My proven strength is intact; I can draw on it. I value relationships more and the quality of interaction. Therefore, I choose friends more wisely. I can touch the depth of others' grief but not take it from them. I am more calm and centered. I can keep my memories and love for Joe while choosing a new life for myself.

WHERE DO I WANT TO GO AND HOW? I choose to continue the positives I've begun: good health habits, nurturing self-talk, pleasure in the moment, quality relationships, etc.

My primary direction, however, is to add more meaning and purpose to my life. I choose to do this by returning to my field of work but selecting a specialty, continuing to write, reconnecting with my family in more mutually fulfilling ways, deepening my religious faith and outreach.

Goals need to be stated in measurable terms. The four areas in the paragraph above each deserve a page where I list specific actions to reach each goal. Easy ways to check progress at specified intervals need to be provided. . . . Then the doing is up to me.

Summary Statement: Have BELIEF in myself, have FAITH in God and HOPE for the future, and then TAKE ACTION.

NEW YEAR'S DAY
Can Be Any Day

I Take Stock:

WHERE HAVE I BEEN?

WHERE AM I NOW?

WHERE DO I WANT TO GO AND HOW?

Summary Statement:

Recommended Reading and Resources

BOOKS

AFTER THE FLOWERS HAVE GONE
Making a Way Out of Grief to a New Life
Bea Decker, as told to Gladys Kooiman
Story of how and why Bea Decker founded THEOS, a national organization for helping the widowed. A book of encouragement and hope.

THE ART OF HUGGING
William Cane
Provides insights needed to add tenderness, know-how, and variety to all kinds of hugs. Includes the "consoling" hug and how to ask for hugs.

THE COMPLETE GUIDE TO HOME SECURITY
How to Protect Your Family and Home from Harm
David Alan Wacker
Includes 19 pages of security product manufacturers and security product catalogs.

CELEBRATE YOUR SELF
Making Life Work for You
Dorothy Corkille Briggs
Published in 1971, still in print, a favorite personal growth book for all times.

*THE COURAGE TO GRIEVE
Creative Living, Recovery & Growth Through Grief
Judy Tatelbaum
Deals with all aspects of grief and its resolution. Easy to read and very practical.

*DON'T TAKE MY GRIEF AWAY
What to Do When You Lose a Loved One
Doug Manning
Thoughtful advice for rebuilding a grief-shattered life while taking to heart the valuable lessons death and mourning impart. Gentle, warm, consoling, and practical.

GETTING THROUGH THE NIGHT
Finding Your Way After the Loss of a Loved One
Eugenia Price
Short, inspirational book written from a Christian perspective.

*GOING SOLO
Widows Tell Their Stories of Love, Loss and Rediscovery
Ted Menten
Ten women honor the past, feel the present, and face the future over coffee and cake.

*THE HEALING POWER OF HUMOR
Techniques for Getting through Loss, Setbacks, Upsets, Disappointments, Difficulties, Trials, Tribulations, and All That Not-So-Funny Stuff
Allen Klein
Provides practical advice on developing humor during times of grief.

*HOW TO SURVIVE THE LOSS OF A LOVE
Melba Colgrove and Harold H. Bloomfield and Peter McWilliams
A best seller. Has 94 suggestions for surviving, healing, and growing.

*I'M GRIEVING AS FAST AS I CAN
How Young Widows and Widowers Can Cope and Heal
Linda Feinberg
Speaks to the unique needs and challenges of the young widowed.

I CAN'T STOP CRYING
It's So Hard When Someone You Love Dies
John D. Martin and Frank D. Ferris
Deals with permission to grieve and suggests steps for rebuilding.

*LIVING WHEN A LOVED ONE HAS DIED
Earl A. Grollman
Gently, honestly, and with simple compassion, the author says what must be said to help confront death and go on living. Easy to read.

A LOOK IN THE MIRROR
A Handbook for Widowers
Edward M. Ames
A widower's story of his return to sounder spirits and increased energy, after he had taken a hard look at himself in the mirror.

MAKING IT THROUGH THE TOUGHEST DAYS OF GRIEF
Anniversaries, Holidays, Other Landmark Days
Meg Woodson
Compassionate and practical advice to see you through these days.

*MEDITATIONS FOR THE WIDOWED
Judy Osgood
Thirty-three men and women offer help for turning hopelessness to hope. They share what enabled them to heal and build new lives for themselves.

*MEN & GRIEF
A Guide for Men Surviving the Death of a Loved One
Carol Staudacher
Helps free men from their uniqueness to deal with their grief.

*MOURNING & MITZVAH
A Guided Journal for Walking the Mourner's Path Through Grief to Healing
Anne Brener
Explores in depth the place where psychology and religious ritual intersect. Many useful activities. Also helpful to those outside the Jewish tradition.

ON DEATH AND DYING
Elizabeth Kübler-Ross
Remains a classic. Dr. Kübler-Ross explores her now-famous five stages of death: denial and isolation, anger, bargaining, depression, and acceptance. Brings hope not only to the dying but to the loved ones who remain.

ON YOUR OWN
A Widow's Passage to Emotional & Financial Well-Being
Alexandra Armstrong and Mary R. Donahue
Authors profile four composite women at ages 43, 50, 62, and 75 to examine different life situations and needs. Very practical help is given.

THE RELAXATION RESPONSE
Herbert Benson
Benson's original simple meditative technique that has helped millions to cope with fatigue, anxiety, and stress. Easy to learn and takes only ten to twenty minutes.

SUDDENLY ALONE
A Woman's Guide to Widowhood
Philomene Gates
Sensitive yet eminently practical book for women learning to cope with the chaos that follows death. Emotional, social, legal, and financial help.

*UNDERSTANDING GRIEF
Helping Yourself Heal
Alan D. Wolfelt
Author creates a safe place for the reader to embrace grief and express it. Not denying, but moving toward the pain of grief, will help heal.

WHAT TO DO WHEN YOUR SPOUSE DIES
Decisions to Make, Legal & Financial Considerations, Planning Ahead
David L. Gibberman
Helpful pamphlet. Order from CCH Inc. by calling 1-800-835-5244.

*WHAT WILL HELP ME? HOW CAN I HELP?
James E. Miller
Book One has 12 suggestions for how to help oneself in grief. Reverse the book for ways to help others who are grieving.

*WHEN WILL I STOP HURTING?
Dealing with a Recent Death
June Cerza Kolf
Author offers creative ways of easing pain and depression in the early days of loss. Grief work continues to the point of letting go and finding out how healing occurs.

*WHY HER WHY NOW
A Man's Journey Through Love and Death and Grief
Lon Elmer
Book of healing in which the author shares his personal journey through the grief experience of losing his wife. Hopeful.

WIDOW
Rebuilding Your Life
Genevieve Ginsburg
A classic that explores every challenge after the death of a mate. Includes a section on the special needs of young widows and widowers, also a survival checklist.

THE WIDOW'S HANDBOOK
A Guide for Living
Charlotte Foehner and Carol Cozart
Deals with the emotional and practical aspects of widowhood. Written in a clear and compassionate way and covers important issues.

*These books may be ordered from:
    Compassion Books
    Rainbow Connection
    477 Hannah Branch Road
    Burnsville, NC 28714

VIDEOS

INVINCIBLE SUMMER
Returning to Life after Someone You Love has Died
17 Minutes, VHS, Color
Teaches the naturalness of the grief process using a meditative blend of words, original music, and stunning
nature photography. Goes through the four seasons.

WHITEWATER
The Positive Power of Grief
22 Minutes, VHS, Color
Uses a metaphor of the rough waters of a fast moving
river to describe critical periods of grief. Viewers are
encouraged to learn navigational skills to eventually
reach calm waters, where the physical presence of a
loved one is felt in memory.

WE WILL REMEMBER
10 Minutes, VHS, Color
Beautiful natural photography, soothing music and
gentle words give permission and encouragement to
use memories of the past for healing in the present. A
memorial.

The above videos may be ordered from:
    Rainbow Connection
    477 Hannah Branch Road
    Burnsville, NC 28714

NEWSLETTER

AFTERLOSS, Inc.
79301 Country Club Drive, Suite 100
Bermuda Dunes, CA 92201
Monthly newsletter that focuses on grief recovery.
1-800-423-8811

ORGANIZATIONS

AMERICAN SELF HELP CLEARING HOUSE
c/o Northwest Covenant Medical Center
25 Pocono Road
Nenville, NJ 07834-2995
201-625-7101
Call to obtain the number of the Clearing House in your
area to locate self-help grief groups near you. Also provides referrals to other national self help organizations.

PARENTS WITHOUT PARTNERS
International Headquarters
401 N. Michigan Avenue
Chicago, IL 60611-4267
1-800-637-7974
Provides educational, social, and family services to single
parents and their children. General information is available.

RECOVERY, INC.
802 North Dearborn Street
Chicago, IL 60610
312-337-5661
An international organization that uses correctly trained
volunteers to lead groups to help persons deal with fears,
depression, and stressful situations. Recovery techniques
and tools are demonstrated at meetings.

THEOS - They Help Each Other Spiritually
322 Boulevard of the Allies, Suite 105
Pittsburgh, PA 15222
412-471 -7779
THEOS provides nondenominational spiritual and educational programs for the widowed and their families.

WIDOWED PERSONS SERVICE (WPS)
AARP/American Association of Retired Persons
601 E Street NW
Washington, DC 20049
202-434-2260
Persons need not be of retirement age or a member of
AARP to benefit from its many services. Local self-help
programs around the country. Bibliographies, pam-
phlets, and many other resources available. Send for a
listing.

MAGAZINE

BEREAVEMENT
A Magazine of Hope and Healing
Bereavement Publishing, Inc.
8133 Telegraph Drive
Colorado Springs, CO 80920-7169
Published six times a year. Stories, articles, and poems are
written by readers who are bereaved themselves. Regular
departments are written by professionals in the field of
grief intervention, addressing many issues. Truly offers
hope and healing.

____
Date

Dear Marta,   MartaFelber@msn.com

____

____

____

____

____

____

____

____

____

____

____

____

____

____

____

____

____

____
(Your Name, Please Print)

____
(Address)

____
(City , State, & Zip)

Marta Felber
P.O. Box 1299
West Fork, AR 72774-1299

Where to Find

ACCEPTANCE, SELF 36, 44, 64, 94

ACTIVITIES 30, 48, 68, 86, 102

ADAPTATION 10, 12, 22, 36, 58, 78, 112

AFFAIRS, LEGAL 66

AFFAIRS, PERSONAL 16, 42, 52, 66

AFFECTION 44, 50

AFFIRMATIONS 40, 44, 64, 94

ALONENESS 10, 22, 24, 58, 60

ANGER 28, 34, 62

ANNIVERSARIES 36, 116

APPEARANCE 80, 90

BEGINNINGS 18, 56, 104, 108, 114, 116

BELIEFS 40, 64, 94, 100

BLESSINGS 40, 56, 100

CELEBRATION 84, 100, 116

CHANGES, MAKING 10, 12, 36, 78, 90, 102, 108, 112

CHOICES 30, 46, 82, 98, 108

COMFORT, FROM OTHERS 20, 26, 52, 56, 106

CONFIDENCE 10, 12, 28, 34, 40, 42, 44, 46, 48, 54, 64,
94, 116

CONTROL, TAKING 12, 14, 16, 28, 30, 34, 36, 38, 46, 48,
54, 58, 66, 74, 78, 82, 90, 102, 116

COURAGE 12, 22, 28, 40, 116

DEATH 18

DECISIONS 16, 82, 96, 108, 116

DIFFICULT SITUATIONS 18, 22, 28, 30, 34, 92, 104, 108,
114

DIRECTIVES 16, 22, 28, 30, 44, 66, 92, 98,

DISASTERS 18, 34, 110

DONATIONS 84, 96

EMPTINESS 10, 24, 58, 60, 78

ENDINGS 18, 66, 72, 92, 114, 116

ENVIRONMENT 10, 12, 24, 78

EXERCISE 14, 74, 90

FAITH 22, 40, 100, 116

FAMILY 52, 66, 116

FEEL GOOD 14, 48, 68, 70, 78, 86, 88, 100, 112, 116

FEELINGS 18, 20, 24, 28, 32, 46, 58, 60, 62, 70, 72, 76, 88,
92, 106, 114

FINANCES 16

FLUCTUATION 108, 110

FORGIVENESS 26, 44, 46, 72

FRIENDS 26, 42, 52, 56, 106

GOALS 14, 74, 90, 98, 102, 116

GOOD-BYES 18, 92, 96, 114

GRIEVING 18, 24, 30, 32, 60, 76, 92, 114

GUIDELINES 28, 36, 82, 98, 102, 106, 116

GUILT 46, 72, 76

HEALTH 14, 74, 90

HELP, PRACTICAL 10, 12, 16, 22, 34, 42, 54, 78, 82, 86,
90, 102

HOME 10, 12, 24, 54, 78

HOMEOWNER 34, 54, 78

HOME MANAGEMENT 34, 42, 54, 78

HONESTY 20, 28, 30, 44, 46, 62, 72

HUGS 50

HURTS 20, 24, 46, 60

JOURNAL WRITING 32

LETTER WRITING 52, 76

LETTING GO 38, 46, 72, 92, 96, 108, 114

LIFE EXTENSION 84, 96, 98

LONELINESS 10, 22, 24, 58, 60

LOOKS, FORWARD 36, 40, 86, 90, 112, 116

MARITAL STATUS 108

MEASUREMENT 16, 110, 112, 116

MEMORIALS 84, 96

MEDITATION 40, 74

MEMORIES 18, 24, 60, 70, 84, 88, 92, 96, 114

MESSAGES 14, 20, 44, 52, 64, 106

MONEY 16

NEEDS 42, 50, 92

NEW LIFE 78, 112, 116

NIGHT TIME 22

NURTURING, SELF 30, 44, 50, 64, 68, 74, 80, 86

OTHERS 20, 26, 42, 52, 56, 66, 106

PLANS, FUTURE 36, 78, 80, 90, 92, 116

POSITIVES 40, 44, 48, 64, 86, 94, 100, 112

PRAYER 22, 74

PROOF 48, 112

PRIORITIES 14, 30, 74, 116

REACHING OUT 42, 50, 52, 56, 116

REALITY 10, 16, 24, 62, 72, 92, 110, 112, 114

RELEASE 32, 38, 46, 62, 72, 76, 92, 114

REPAIRS 34, 54

RESENTMENTS 20, 28, 62

RESOURCES, READING, AND ORGANIZATIONS 119

SAFETY, PERSONAL 12, 28, 38

SECURITY 12, 28, 42, 54

SELF-ESTEEM 44, 64, 68, 80, 94, 116

SELF-TALK 44, 46, 64, 94

SERVICE PERSONS 42, 54

SEX 104

SEXUALITY 28, 104, 108

SINGLE STATUS 108

SLEEP 14, 22, 74

STRENGTH, GAINING 28, 30, 40, 44, 46, 48, 64, 94, 100

STRESS RELEASE 14, 22, 34, 44, 74

STRUCTURE, ADDING 14, 16, 40, 48, 74, 102

SUPPORT 26, 42, 44, 56

SURVIVAL 22, 32, 110, 116

THANKFULNESS 100, 116

TIME MANAGEMENT 102

TOOLS 54, 96

TRAITS, POSITIVE 44, 64, 90, 94, 98

TREATS 50, 68, 80, 86

TRIBUTES 84, 96, 98

UNDERSTANDING, SELF 28, 44, 46, 64, 72, 94, 104, 108, 106

VISUALIZATION 60, 64, 94

WARMTH 50, 88, 106

WIDOWED 108

WORRIES 12, 16, 38, 74

WRITING, SOLUTIONS THROUGH 10, 12, 22, 32, 82

YOUTH REGAINED 90

ORDER FORM

LifeWords
P.O. Box 1299
West Fork, AR 72774-1299
MartaFelber@msn.com

(FOR CREDIT CARD ORDERS ONLY)
FAX: 501-839-8384
1-800-798-0100

❶ CUSTOMER'S PHONE: DAY _______________________ EVENING _______________________

❷ ORDERED BY:

NAME _______________________

ADDRESS _______________________

CITY, STATE, & ZIP _______________________

    Please ship _________ copies of (Regular Edition) to this address

    Please ship _________ copies of (*Deluxe Gift Edition) to this address

❸ SHIP TO:

IF DIFFERENT FROM ABOVE ADDRESS

NAME _______________________

ADDRESS _______________________

CITY, STATE, & ZIP _______________________

    Please ship _________ copies of (Regular Edition) to this address

    Please ship _________ copies of (*Deluxe Gift Edition) to this address

❹ GIFT ADDRESS:

NAME _______________________

ADDRESS _______________________

CITY, STATE, & ZIP _______________________

    Please ship _________ copies of (Regular Edition) to this address

    Please ship _________ copies of (*Deluxe Gift Edition) to this address

☐ Enclose a gift card to read: _______________________
____

Signed _______________________

❺ ITEMS ORDERED:

QUANTITY	TITLE	PRICE	AMOUNT
	Grief Expressed: When a Mate Dies (Regular Edition) ISBN 0-9653967-4-6	$19.95	$
	Grief Expressed: When a Mate Dies (*Deluxe Gift Edition) ISBN 0-9653967-3-8	$24.95	$

SHIPPING CHARGES

First book $3.00. Each additional book $.75. For international orders, please add an additional $4.00 per order.

SUBTOTAL	$
LESS 10% FOR ORDERS OF 10 COPIES	$( )
SUBTOTAL	$
ARKANSAS RESIDENTS ADD 5.5% SALES TAX	$
SHIPPING & HANDLING	$
INTERNATIONAL ORDERS SHIPPING & HANDLING	$
TOTAL ORDER	$

❻ METHOD OF PAYMENT:

☐ CHECK / MONEY ORDER

☐ MASTER CARD   ☐ VISA

CARD NUMBER _______________________

EXPIRATION DATE _______________________ SIGNATURE _______________________

CARD MEMBER'S NAME (PRINT) _______________________

** The Deluxe Gift Edition is bound in a European style cover (with extended cover flaps) and is packaged in a gold foil-stamped sleeve.*